The Best of *The Mailbox®* Magazine

Centers & Games

The best centers and games from the 2005–2010 issues of *The Mailbox®* magazine

- Punctuation
- Prefixes and suffixes
- Spelling
- Comprehension
- Writing
- Number sense
- Place value
- Computation
- Fractions
- Measurement

Editorial Team: Becky S. Andrews, Debbie Ashworth, Diane Badden, Kimberley Bruck, Karen A. Brudnak, Pam Crane, Chris Curry, Tazmen Hansen, Marsha Heim, Lori Z. Henry, Kitty Lowrance, Gerri Primak, Mark Rainey, Greg D. Rieves, Hope Rodgers-Medina, Rebecca Saunders, Donna K. Teal, Sharon M. Tresino, Zane Williard

www.themailbox.com

ISBN 978-1-61276-215-9

Printed in the United States
10 9 8 7 6 5 4 3 2 1

HPS233484

Table of Contents

Language Arts Centers 3

Activities 4

Full-color centers 13

Reproducibles 19

Math Centers 27

Activities 28

Full-color centers 37

Reproducibles 43

Language Arts Games 51

Activities 52

Full-color games 61

Reproducibles 67

Math Games 73

Activities 74

Full-color games 83

Reproducibles 87

Answer Keys 94

Skills Index 96

Language Arts CENTERS

Language Arts CENTERS

Stacking Up Words

Onsets and rimes

This matching center has students pairing rimes with onsets. To prepare, program five foam cups with rimes as shown. In addition, program ten other cups, each with a different one of the listed onsets. Then place the cups at a center with a supply of paper. A child matches two onset cups with each rime cup by stacking them as shown. Then on a sheet of paper, she writes the words the onsets and rimes make.

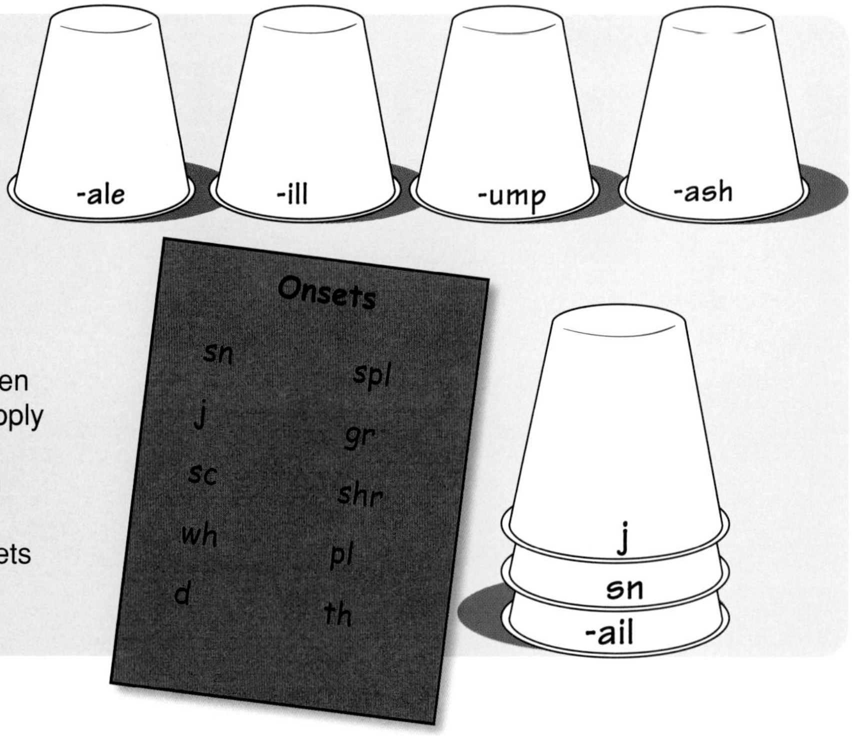

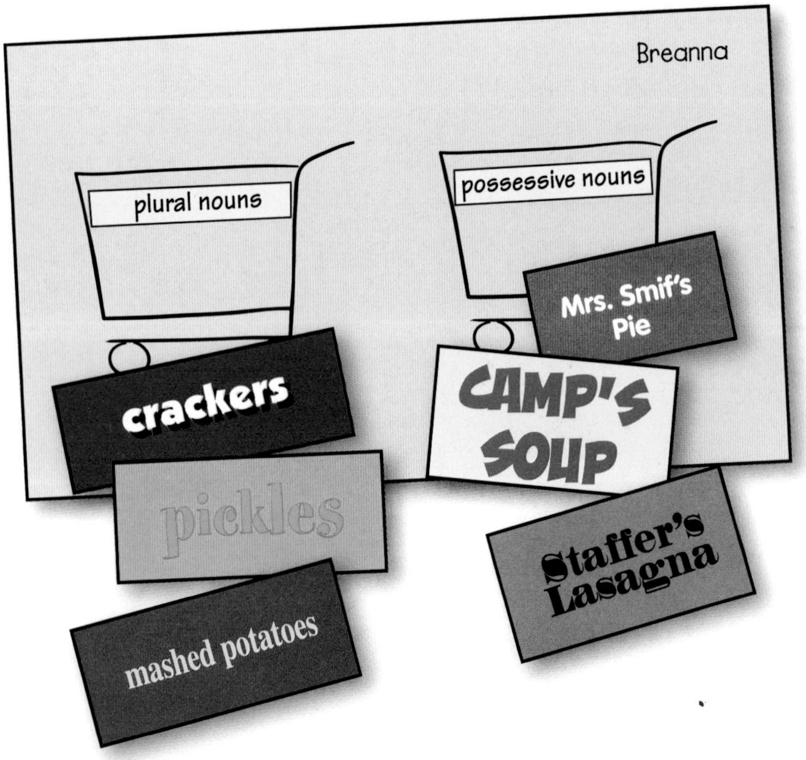

Shopping for Examples

Plural nouns

This easy-to-prepare center helps students recognize plural and possessive nouns. Collect a variety of food labels and place them in a paper bag. Place the bag at a center with a supply of blank paper and cards labeled like the ones shown. A child reads the parts of speech on the cards and then draws two shopping cart shapes on her paper. She places a card on each cart; then she refers to the products' names as she sorts the labels onto the corresponding carts. If a label does not match one of the parts of speech, she sets it aside. After she's sorted the labels, the student writes the product names in a two-column chart on another sheet of paper.

Renee Green
Hooper Bay School
Hooper Bay, AK

Spelling Box
Spelling

Help students practice sounding out and spelling words! In advance, cut out a variety of magazine pictures featuring objects whose names you want students to practice spelling. Glue each picture to one side of a blank index card and write the word on the opposite side. Store the cards in a box and place it at a center along with a small dry-erase board and a wipe-off marker. A student selects a card and looks at the picture. She sounds out the word and writes it on her board. Then she flips the card over to check her work. She continues drawing cards and spelling words for as long as desired.

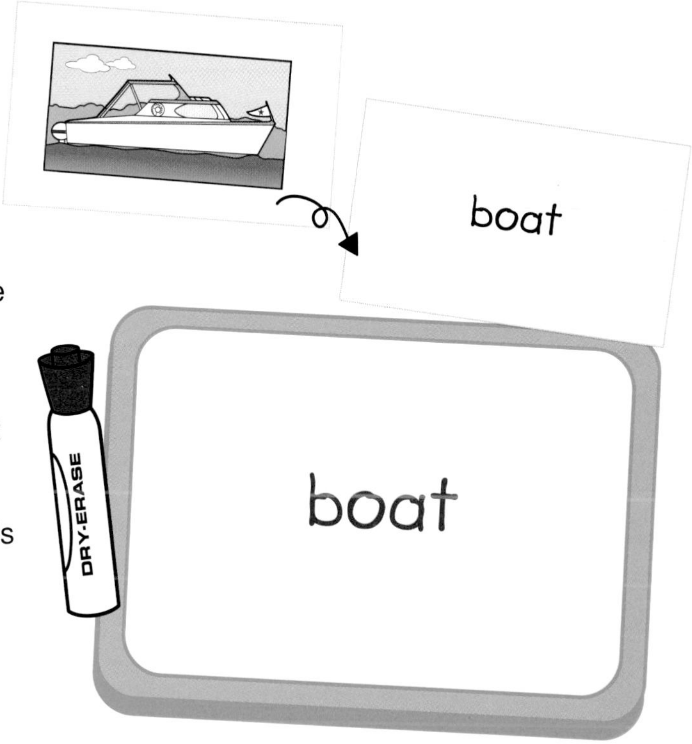

Melinda Folson
St. James the Less School
Columbus, OH

"Egg-cellent" Practice
Spelling

With minimal preparation, this spelling activity can be used all year long! Color a copy of the center mat on page 19. Laminate the mat and use a permanent marker to write the scrambled letters of a different spelling word on each yolk. Also write the corresponding spelling words on the toaster. Place the mat, a dry-erase marker, and paper towels at a center. A child follows the directions on the mat to unscramble and write each word. When the student has unscrambled all ten words, she wipes the mat clean. To prepare the mat for a new list of words, use rubbing alcohol to wipe away the permanent marker.

Colleen Reninger
Worth Elementary
Worth, IL

Ready to Read

Sight words

To help student pairs bravely conquer sight words, make several copies of the knight pattern and word strip on page 20 and cut them out. Program each section of a strip with a sight word, making strips of different words. If desired, laminate the patterns for durability. Next, cut two slits on each knight's shield and feed a strip through the slits. Glue or tape the ends together and place the completed knights at a center. A child chooses a knight and reads each word to a partner by slowly pulling the back side of the strip. When she correctly reads all ten words, she chooses another knight and repeats the process. After correctly reading two strips, partners trade roles.

Phyllis Steinberg
Wheelock Primary School
Fredonia, NY

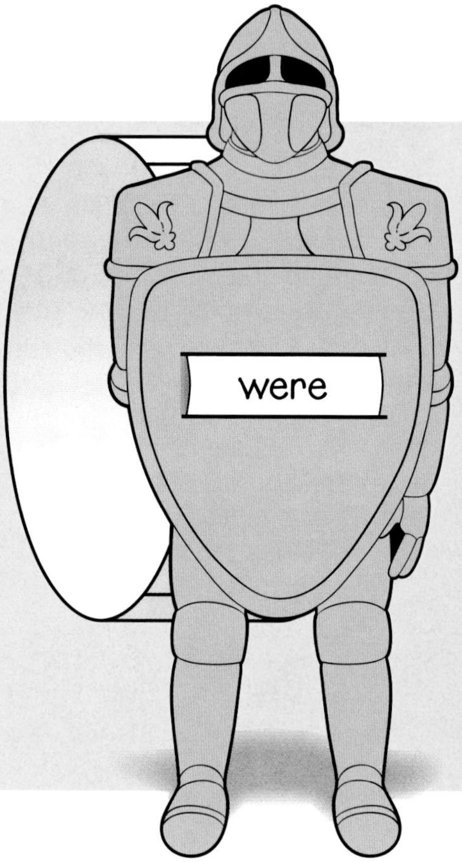

Angler Action

Capitalizing places, holidays, special events, and times in history

Fishing for correct capital letters is the focus of this center activity. Cut out the mat and cards on page 13; then place them at a center. A child decides whether each card uses correct capitalization and places it on the corresponding space on the mat. Then she flips the cards over to check her work. If time allows, she correctly writes each incorrect card on a sheet of paper.

Mederise Burke
Courthouse Road Elementary
Spotsylvania, VA

Magic Beans

Adding missing commas

Write on several sentence strips a variety of sentences or phrases with missing commas, like the ones shown. Place the strips at a center along with a handful of dried beans, paper, and pencils. A child selects a sentence strip, reads it, and uses the beans to add commas where needed. Then he copies the correctly punctuated sentence onto a sheet of paper. He repeats the process for as long as desired.

Jean Erickson
Grace Christian Academy
West Allis, WI

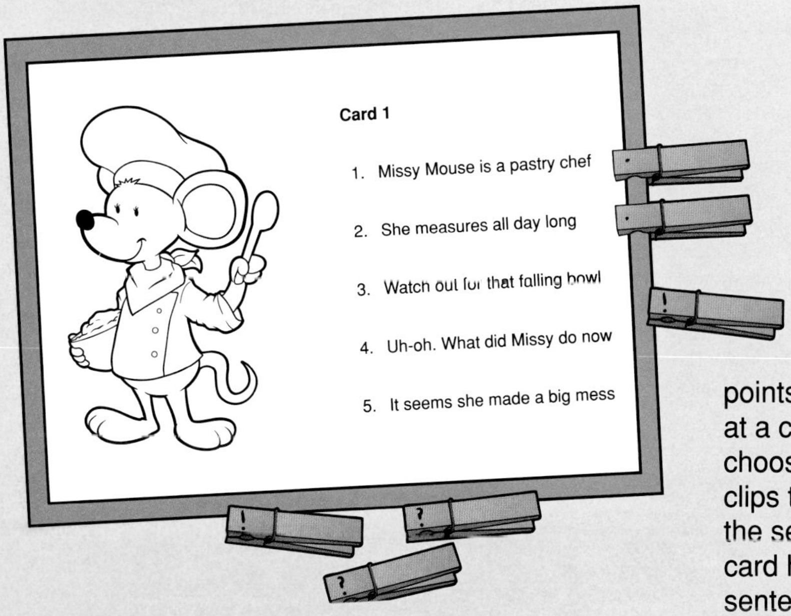

End of the Line

Using correct end marks

To provide independent practice using end marks, copy the cards on page 21 and cut them out. Mount the cards on construction paper and laminate them for durability. Also program two clothespins with periods, two with question marks, and two with exclamation points. Place the cards and clothespins at a center with a supply of paper. A child chooses a card, reads a sentence, and clips the correct clothespin at the end of the sentence. When each sentence on the card has been punctuated, he copies the sentences onto his paper and writes the correct end marks.

adapted from an idea by Bonnie Gaynor
Franklin, NJ

They're There!

Homophones

To prepare the center, copy page 22 to make a homophone pair for each student. Place the cards at a center along with paper strips, glue, and crayons. A child chooses a homophone pair and glues each card to a paper strip. For each word, he writes across the bottom of the paper a sentence using the word and illustrates the sentence at the top. When each child has completed a pair, hang the sets alphabetically for an instant word wall reference!

Allison Russell
Gleason Elementary
Houston, TX

Colorful Endings

Inflectional endings

Word-building skills are hatched at this independent center. To prepare, copy the list of inflectional endings shown, cut the endings apart, and then place each one inside a different plastic egg. Display the eggs at a center along with a list of base words. The child removes a word ending from an egg, adds it to the first base word on the list, and then writes the new word on his paper. He continues with each word on his list.

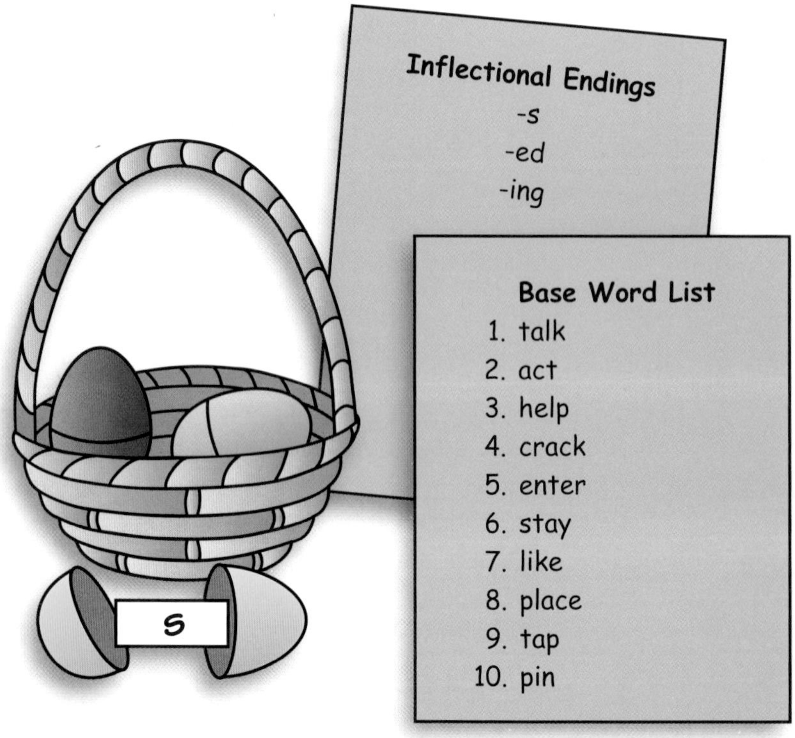

Tina Alvear
Julian Gibson Elementary
Winston-Salem, NC

Rolled Into One

Prefixes

This partner center helps students build a vocabulary of words with prefixes. Cut out and assemble a tagboard copy of the cube pattern from page 23. Also make copies of the recording sheet from the same page and the answer key on page 94. Working with a partner, a student rolls the cube and reads the top-facing prefix. He locates a base word on the recording sheet that, when added to the prefix, makes a real word and writes the prefix by the base word in his column. To confirm his choice, the child uses the word in a sentence and checks the answer key. He marks a check in the box if it is correct and an X if it is not correct. Then the other player takes a turn in the same manner. Students alternate turns until a prefix has been added to each base word or time runs out.

Carolyn M. Burant, St. John Vianney School, Brookfield, WI

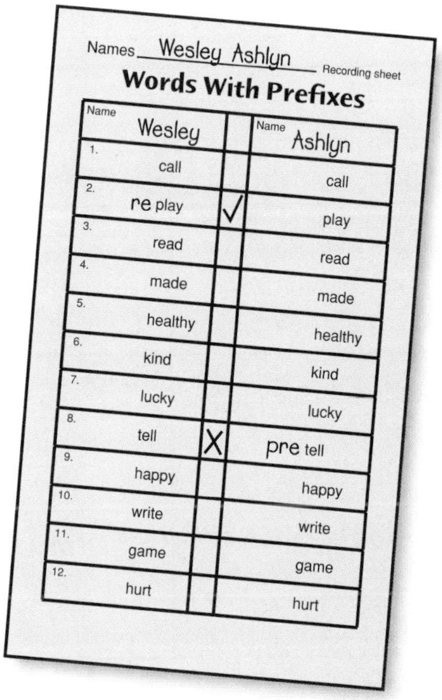

Names Wesley Ashlyn   Recording sheet

Words With Prefixes

Name Wesley		Name Ashlyn
1. call		call
2. re play	✓	play
3. read		read
4. made		made
5. healthy		healthy
6. kind		kind
7. lucky		lucky
8. tell	X	pre tell
9. happy		happy
10. write		write
11. game		game
12. hurt		hurt

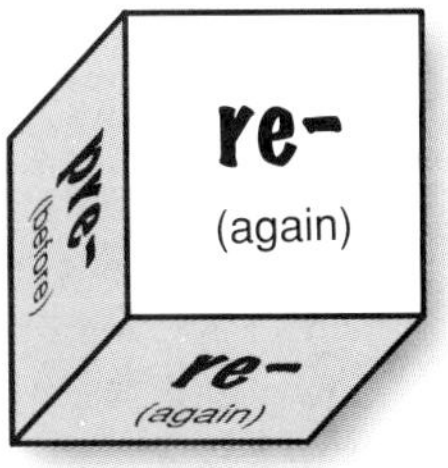

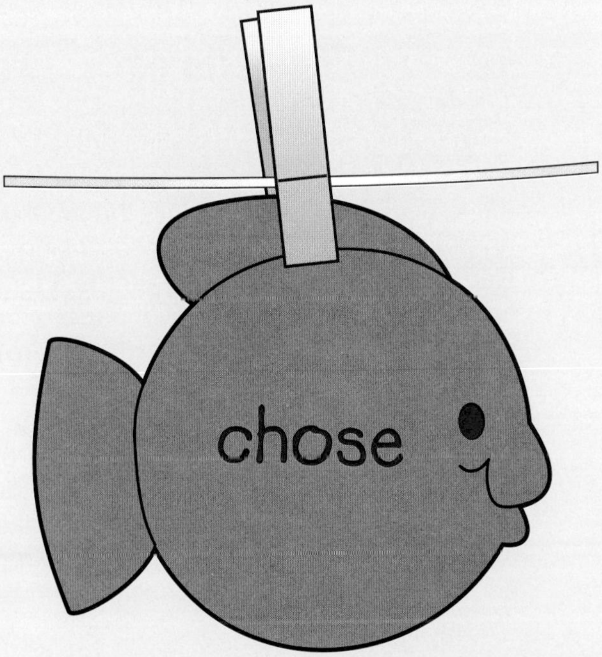

Tackling the Alphabet

ABC order

What's the catch of the day at this center? Improved alphabetizing skills! Label a supply of fish cutouts with spelling or vocabulary words. Laminate the fish and cut them out. Store the fish and a supply of clothespins in a small tackle or pencil box. Also hang a length of fishing line along a wall or under a bulletin board. Place the tackle box near the fishing line along with paper and pencils. A student uses the clothespins to attach the fish to the line in alphabetical order. After he finishes arranging the words, he writes them in alphabetical order on his paper.

Sondra Alexander
Mobile County Public Schools
Mobile, AL

! See page 15 for a colorful sorting center on SUFFIXES!

Language Arts CENTERS

Dig In

Writing

Students will be eager to plow through this question-writing activity. Cut out seasonal pictures, like the ones shown, from newspapers and magazines. Store the pictures in a bucket and place it at a center with glue, paper, and pencils. A student selects a picture and glues it to his paper. Then he writes three questions about the picture. If time allows, he uses visual cues and his own prior experiences to provide possible answers.

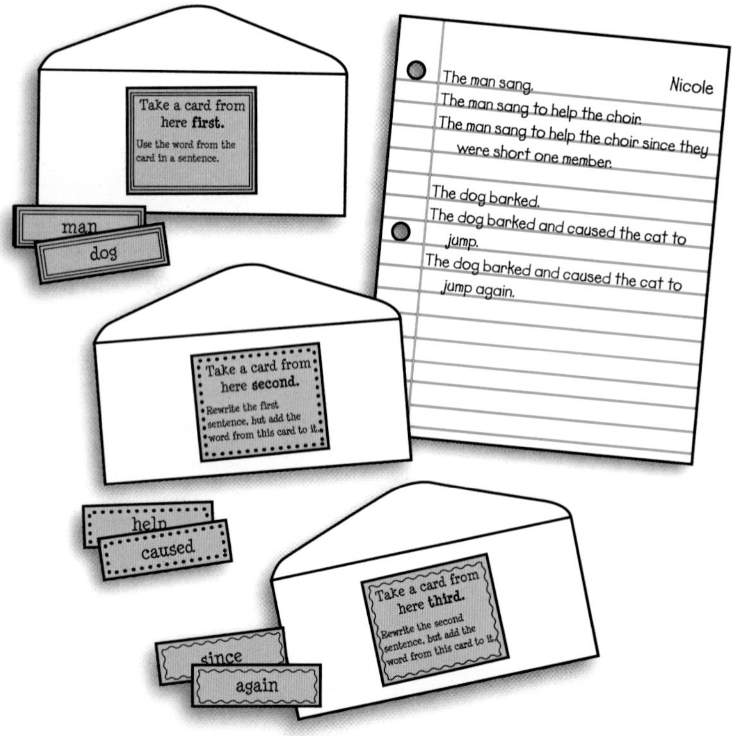

Take Three

Writing

To deliver descriptive writing practice with a twist, copy page 24 and cut apart the left column of cards. Glue the label to an envelope and place the cards inside. Repeat with the other two columns. Place the envelopes and a supply of paper at a center. A student selects a card from the first envelope and writes a simple sentence that uses the word. Next, the child takes a card from the second envelope, copies the first sentence, and extends it by using the newly chosen word. Finally, the child takes a card from the last envelope, copies the second sentence, and extends it by adding the final word.

Louella Nygaard
Mount Eccles Elementary
Cordova, AK

Salad Sort

Word order

Students improve their sentence skills at this center! In advance, write several sentences, each on a different-colored sentence strip. (If desired, use colors found in a salad, such as green, red, or orange.) Cut each strip, leaving one word on each piece. Toss the pieces into a plastic bowl and place it at a center along with paper and pencils. First, a student sorts the pieces by color. Next, he chooses a set of color cards and arranges them to form a complete sentence. He repeats the process for each remaining set of cards. Then he writes the sentences he formed on a sheet of paper and returns the cards to the bowl.

Snip and Sort

Details from text

At this literacy center, students identify and organize important details they read in nonfiction books. Stock a center with nonfiction books, student copies of page 25, paper, scissors, and glue. A child reads a book and then writes on a copy of page 25 a different important detail on each card. Next, the student writes the book's title and author's name at the top of a sheet of paper. He cuts out the cards and groups them in an arrangement that makes sense to him. Then he glues them to his paper and labels each group.

Lisa Russo
Flushing, NY

On a Roll
Comprehension

This center activity gets students rolling with comprehension! Cut out the dice on page 17. Fold each one on the dotted lines and then tape or glue the sides together at the tabs to form a die. Place the completed dice at a center with paper and pencils and a key like the one shown. A child visits the center and selects the die that corresponds with his reading selection. He labels his paper with his name and the name of his book. He rolls the die and then writes on his paper the question's number and his answer. He repeats the process three times. Collect students' papers to check their comprehension.

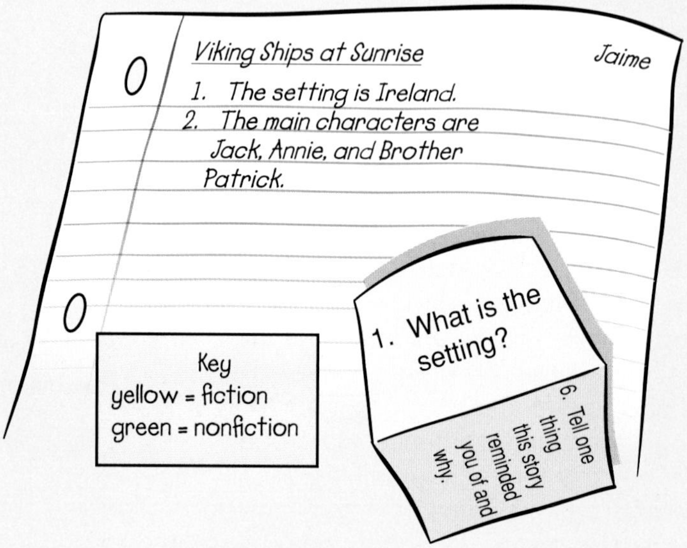

Piper R. Porter
Mountain Way Elementary
Granite Falls, WA

On the Page
Text-to-text connections

Stock a center with a class supply of copies of page 26 and several books on the same topic, in the same series, of the same genre, or by the same author. At the center, each student reads the books for a set amount of time. Then the child chooses one book. She writes about the book as guided on the left side of her reproducible. Next, the student chooses another book from her reading, thinks about the connections between the books, and records her ideas on the right side of the page. Follow up by having each student share her connections with a partner.

Dr. Jennifer L. Kohnke
St. Charles, IL

Use with "Angler Action" on page 6.

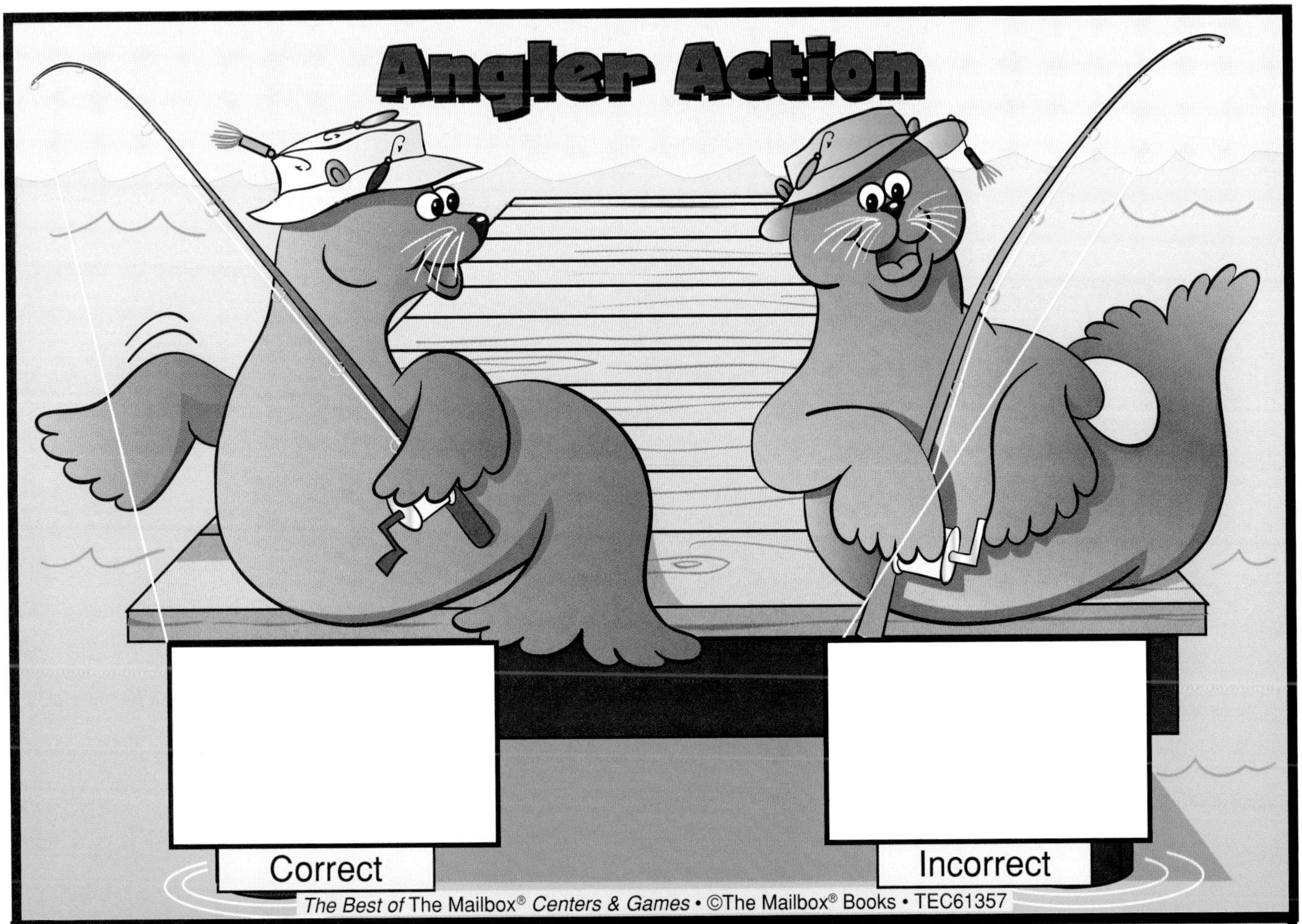

father's day	Lake travis	gulf of Mexico	fleet week
Rock Creek	Pacific Ocean	thanksgiving	Mother's Day
New year's Day	Civil War	red River	Millers Pond
Egypt	middle ages	Labor day	Autumn Moon Festival

X TEC61357	X TEC61357	X TEC61357	X TEC61357
✓ TEC61357	X TEC61357	✓ TEC61357	✓ TEC61357
✓ TEC61357	X TEC61357	✓ TEC61357	X TEC61357
✓ TEC61357	X TEC61357	X TEC61357	✓ TEC61357

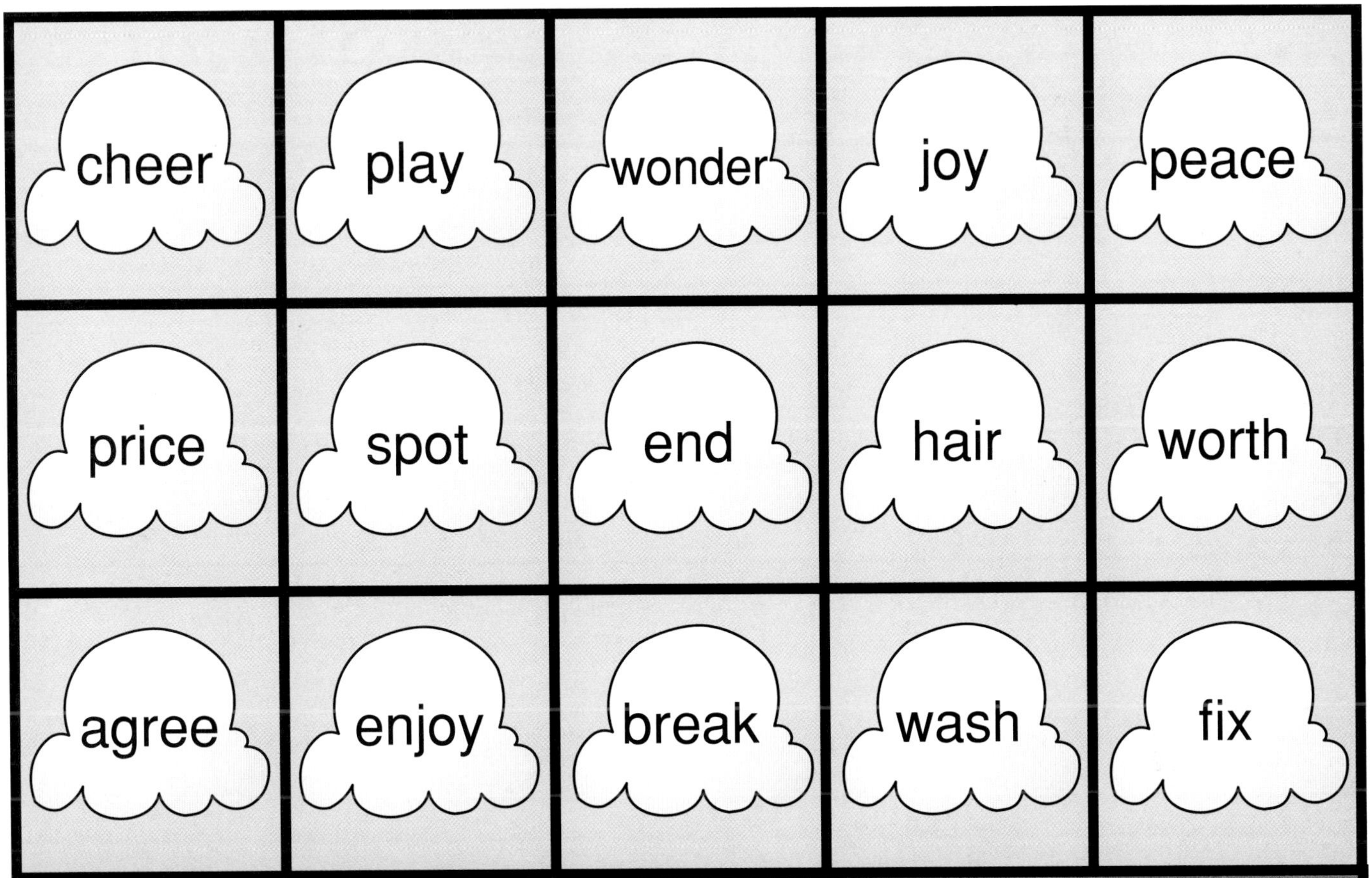

Note to the Teacher: Mount the cards and mat on construction paper; cut them out. Place the cards and mat at a center. A child sorts each card by placing it on the suffix that, when combined with the base word, forms a new word. After sorting the cards he turns them over to check his work.

-ful TEC61357	-ful TEC61357	-ful TEC61357	-ful TEC61357	-ful TEC61357
-less TEC61357	-less TEC61357	-less TEC61357	-less TEC61357	-less TEC61357
-able TEC61357	-able TEC61357	-able TEC61357	-able TEC61357	-able TEC61357

Use with "On a Roll" on page 12.

1. What is the setting?
2. Who are the main characters?
3. What is the problem?
4. What is the solution?
5. Tell about the beginning, middle, and end of the story.
6. Tell one thing this story reminded you of and why.

1. What is the main idea?
2. Name two supporting details.
3. What is the purpose of the book? How can you tell?
4. Briefly summarize the book.
5. Why is this topic important?
6. Tell one thing this book reminded you of and why.

TEC61357

TEC61357

"Egg-cellent" Practice

Unscramble the letters.
Write the spelling word on the line.
Cross off the matching word on the toaster.

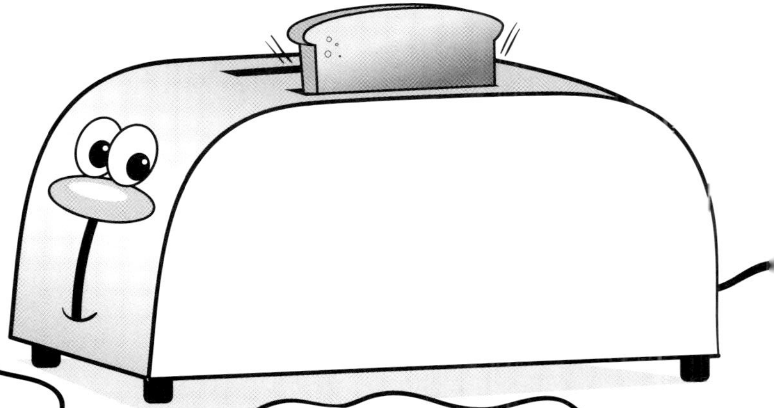

Note to the teacher: Use with "'Egg-cellent' Practice" on page 5.

Knight Pattern and Word Strip

Use with "Ready to Read" on page 6.

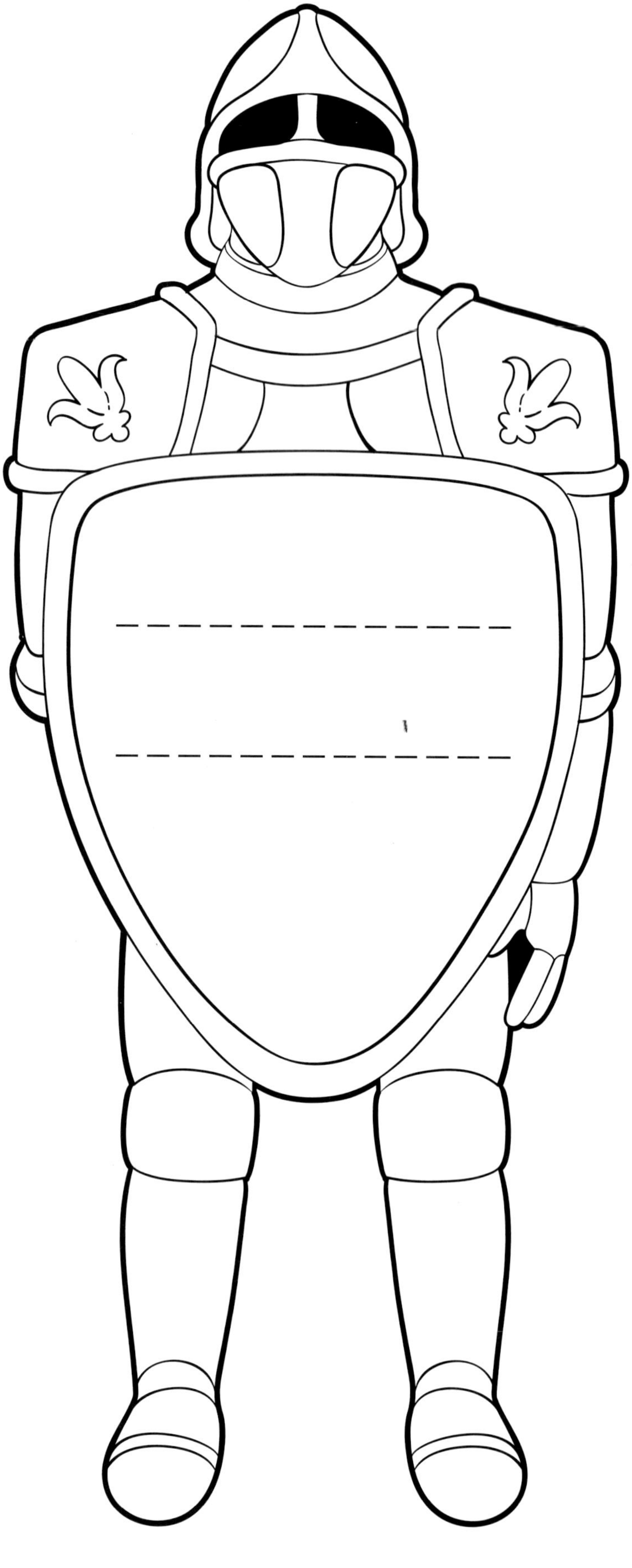

Glue.

TEC61357

"Egg-cellent" Practice

Unscramble the letters.
Write the spelling word on the line.
Cross off the matching word on the toaster.

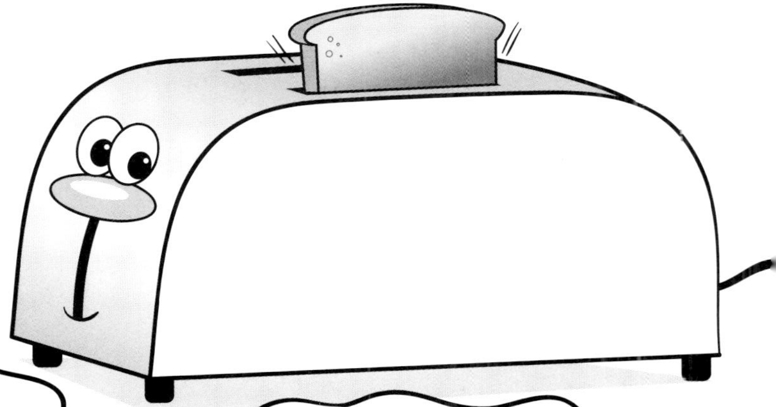

Note to the teacher: Use with "'Egg-cellent' Practice" on page 5.

Knight Pattern and Word Strip

Use with "Ready to Read" on page 6.

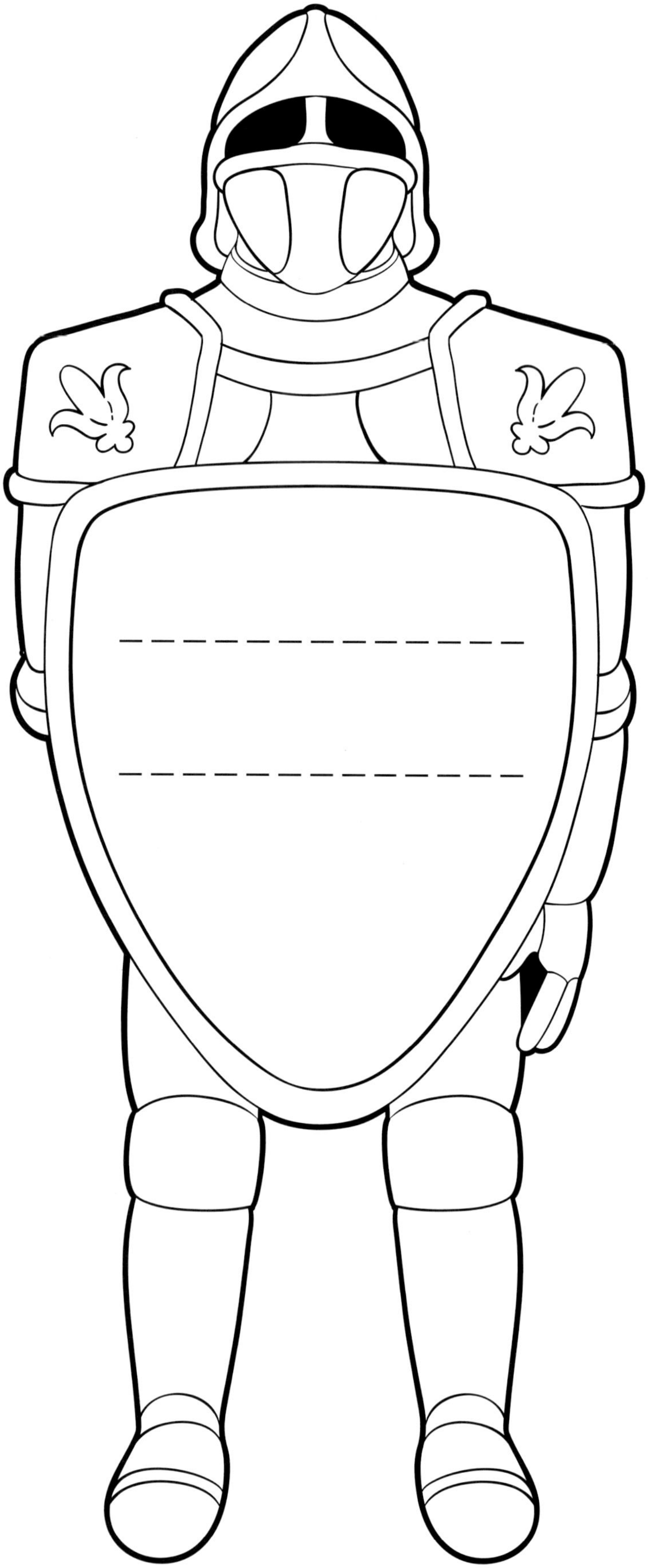

Use with "End of the Line" on page 7.

Card 1

1. Missy Mouse is a pastry chef
2. She measures all day long
3. Watch out for that falling bowl
4. Uh-oh. What did Missy do now
5. It seems she made a big mess

TEC61357

Card 2

1. Have you heard about Martin Mouse
2. He loves to build fun mazes
3. He has become famous for them
4. Martin can build a maze in just five minutes
5. What do you think his secret is

TEC61357

Homophone Cards

Use with "They're There!" on page 8.

ate TEC61357	eight TEC61357	buy TEC61357	bye TEC61357
stare TEC61357	stair TEC61357	hole TEC61357	whole TEC61357
one TEC61357	won TEC61357	nose TEC61357	knows TEC61357
right TEC61357	write TEC61357	rose TEC61357	rows TEC61357
tail TEC61357	tale TEC61357	tea TEC61357	tee TEC61357
toad TEC61357	towed TEC61357	waist TEC61357	waste TEC61357

Use with "Rolled Into One" on page 9.

Names________ Recording sheet

Words With Prefixes

Name		Name
1. call		call
2. play		play
3. read		read
4. made		made
5. healthy		healthy
6. kind		kind
7. lucky		lucky
8. tell		tell
9. happy		happy
10. write		write
11. game		game
12. hurt		hurt

To assemble the cube, cut along the bold lines. Fold on each thin line and glue it together using the resulting flaps.

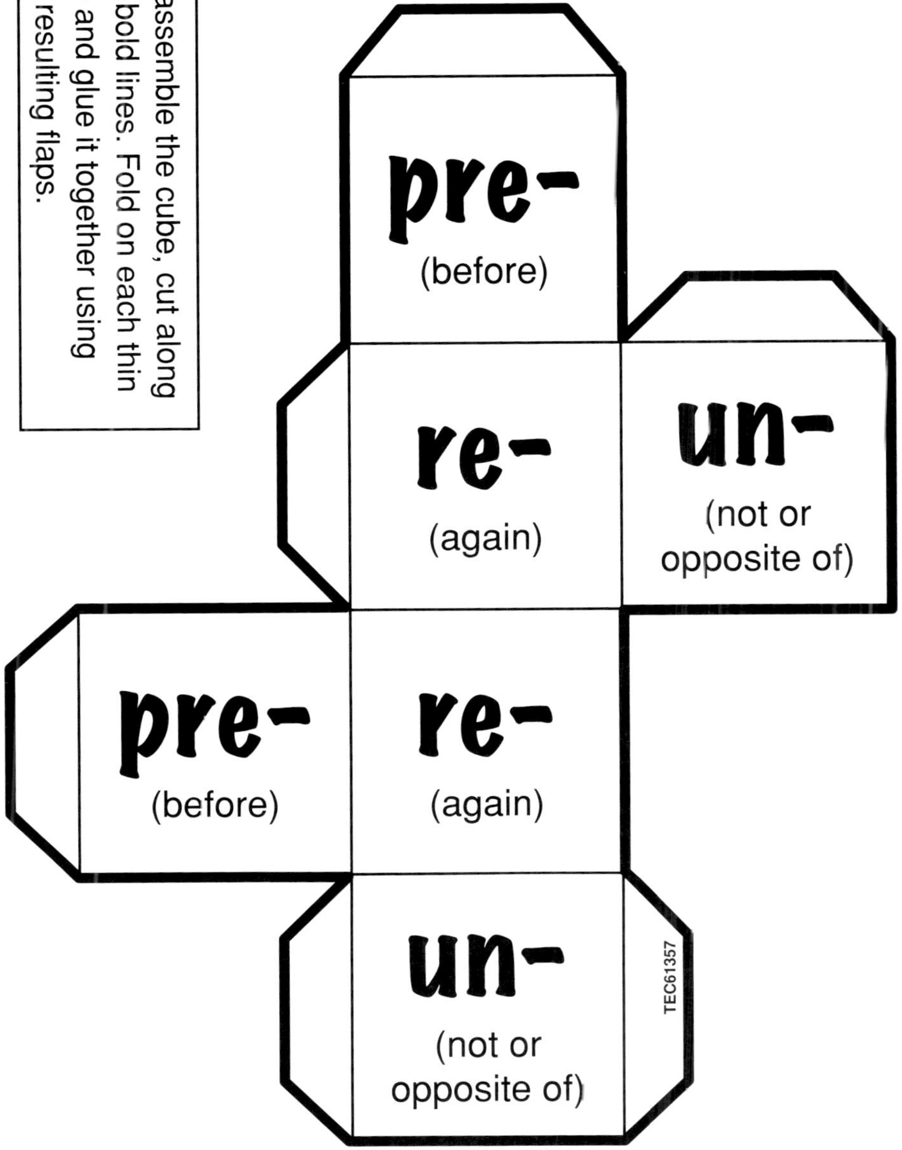

Labels and Word Cards

Use with "Take Three" on page 10.

Take a card from here **first.** Use the word from the card in a sentence. TEC61357	Take a card from here **second.** Rewrite the first sentence, but add the word from this card to it. TEC61357	Take a card from here **third.** Rewrite the second sentence, but add the word from this card to it. TEC61357
people TEC61357	used TEC61357	again TEC61357
parakeet TEC61357	said TEC61357	don't TEC61357
man TEC61357	write TEC61357	dribble TEC61357
boy TEC61357	make TEC61357	thump TEC61357
lady TEC61357	find TEC61357	crash TEC61357
mother TEC61357	gave TEC61357	stand TEC61357
father TEC61357	help TEC61357	air TEC61357
dog TEC61357	caused TEC61357	along TEC61357
friend TEC61357	moved TEC61357	since TEC61357
story TEC61357	follow TEC61357	without TEC61357

TEC61357

TEC61357

TEC61357

TEC61357

TEC61357

TEC61357

TEC61357

TEC61357

From One to Another

Note to the teacher: Use with “On the Page” on page 12.

Math CENTERS

Math CENTERS

Memorable Facts

Adding doubles and near doubles

To prepare this center for two, remove the face cards and aces from a deck of playing cards. Player 1 shuffles the deck and places each card facedown on the workspace. Player 2 turns over two cards, looking for a set of doubles (5 + 5) or near-doubles (5 + 6 or 4 + 5). If she makes a match, she states its sum and places the cards in her own stack. If desired, have Player 2 check Player 1's answers with a calculator or hundred chart. If a match is not made, the cards are turned over in their original locations. Player 2 takes a turn in a similar manner and play continues until all possible matches have been made.

Stacie Wright
Millington School
Millington, NJ

Number Jewels

Using < and >

Comparing numbers is a cinch with this center activity! Make one or more copies of the jewel patterns and greater- and less-than cards on page 43 on colored construction paper. Cut out the jewels and store them in a container that resembles a treasure chest. Place the chest, symbol cards, paper, and pencils at a center. A child removes the jewels from the chest and uses them to create two three-digit numbers. He arranges his numbers beside each other, as shown, and chooses the correct symbol to place between them to make the number sentence true. Then he copies the number sentence onto a sheet of paper. He repeats the process until he has created ten different number sentences and written them on his paper.

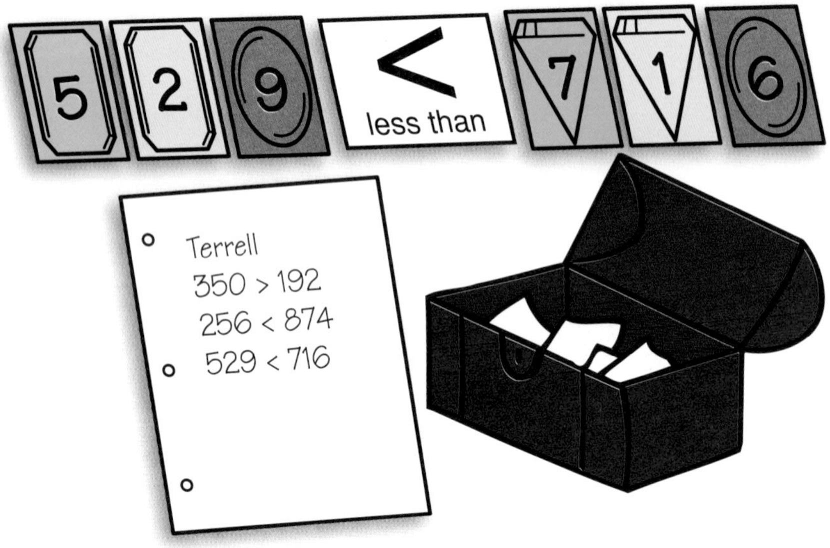

Results Will Vary

Computation skills

Program two sets of cards: one set with the numbers 1–5 and the other set with numbers that are answers to grade-appropriate addition, subtraction, multiplication, or division problems. Put each set in a separate resealable bag and label the bags as shown. A child chooses a card from each bag. He uses the card drawn from the "Problems" bag to determine the number of problems he must write that result in the answer found on the other card. After he records his answers, he returns the cards to the bags; then he selects a new pair.

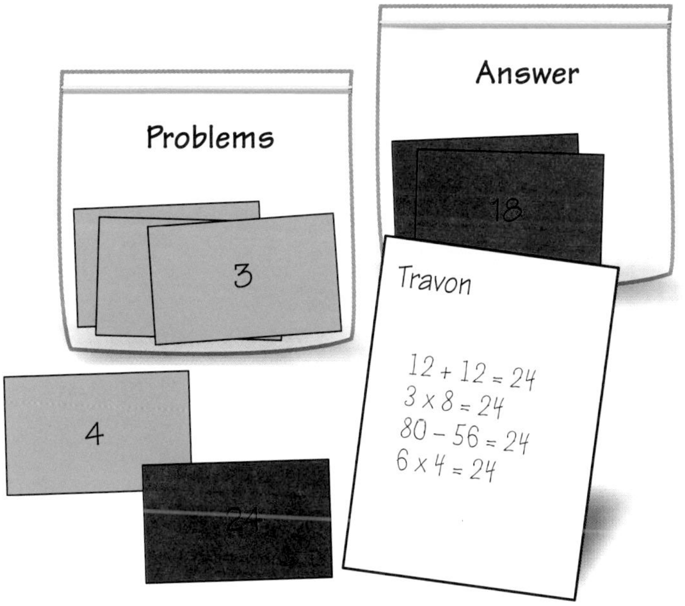

Jackpot!

Multiplication

For this partner center, program a supply of paper strips with three different products on each. Also write each number from 1 to 10 on two sets of index cards and store them in a paper lunch bag. Place the bag and strips at a center with a supply of game markers and a calculator. To play, Player 1 takes a strip and randomly selects two cards from the bag. She multiplies the numbers and names the product. Player 2 confirms Player 1's answer, using the calculator as needed. If Player 1 is correct and her product matches one of the numbers on the strip, she covers it with a game marker before placing the cards back in the bag. Then Player 2 takes a turn in a similar manner. The player to cover the last number says "jackpot" and wins the round. Then the duo plays again with another strip.

adapted from an idea by David Green
North Shore Country Day School
Winnetka, IL

Math CENTERS

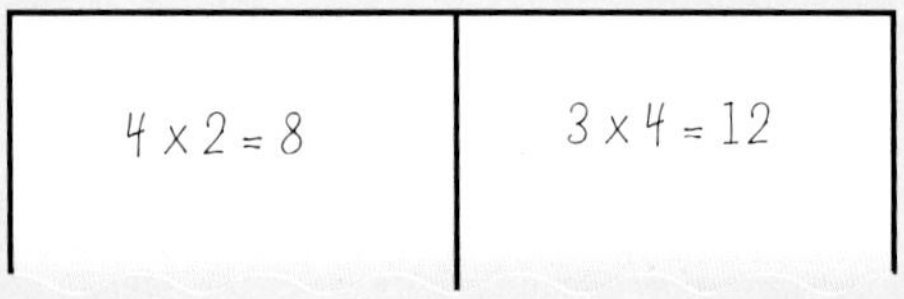

Three Times the Fun

Multiplication

To prepare, place five dice in a paper cup and store the cup at a center with a supply of paper and pencils. A child folds a sheet of paper in half three times and then unfolds the paper to reveal eight sections. She rolls the dice and sets aside any with matching amounts. Then she returns the remaining dice to the cup, rolls again, and keeps any dice matching those from the first roll. She repeats the process a third time; then she uses the number of dice and the repeated number on each to write a multiplication problem in one section of her paper. If necessary, she uses the dots on the dice to help her solve it. She repeats the steps to create seven more problems.

Jennifer Thoutt
Edmondson Elementary
Loveland, CO

Sunny Facts

Multiplication

Copy page 44 on yellow paper; then cut out the cards. Write a multiplication problem on the top of each sun and its answer on the bottom. Program the backs of matching cards with same-colored dots for self-checking and then place them at a center. A child matches each problem to its answer. Then she turns the cards over to check her work.

Patricia Frano
Meadville, PA

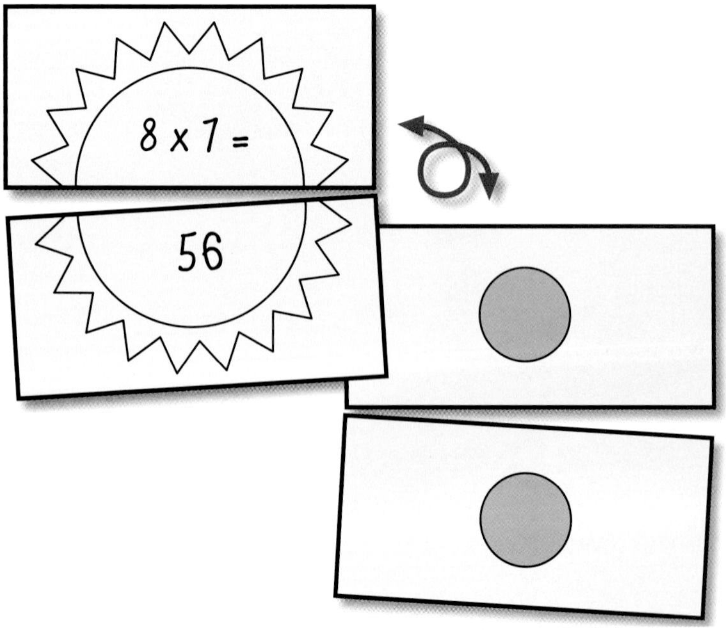

! See page 37 for a DIVISION Center!

Tools for Work

Place value

Cut apart the cards on page 39. Store the cards in an empty crayon box at a center. A child places each crayon below the box that matches the value of its underlined digit. After flipping over the cards to check his answers, he writes each set of cards as a separate list on a sheet of paper.

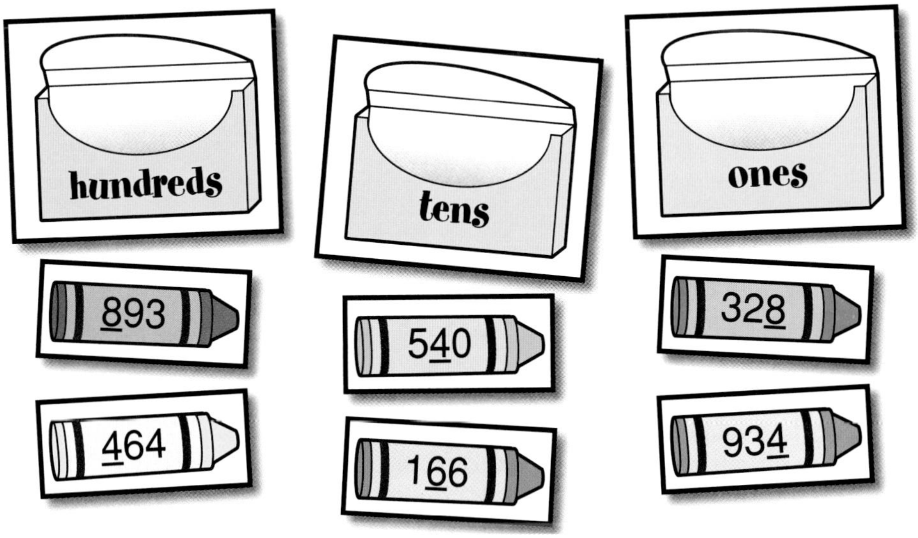

Peekaboo Numbers

Expanded form

Visualizing numbers in standard and expanded form is as easy as 1, 2, 3! In advance, cut a supply of sentence strips in half, making enough for each child to have two. Place the sentence strips and a die at a center. A child rolls the die and writes the number as the hundreds digit at the far left end of a sentence strip as shown. He repeats the process, writing the second number as the tens digit in the middle and the last number as the ones digit at the far right. Next, he fills in the value for each digit and adds plus signs where needed. He folds the first and last digits back and then creases the folded ends of the strip toward the tens digit. He reads the number with the strip closed and then opens the strip to reveal the number in expanded form. He repeats the process to show a new number with expanded and standard form.

Amanda Darmo
New Town Elementary
Owings Mills, MD

Math CENTERS

Story Problem Scenes

Problem solving

Use these math story starters to provide practice with writing and solving word problems. Cut apart several copies of the cards from page 45; then place them at a center with crayons, glue, and a supply of paper. A child selects a card and adds illustrations as directed. Next, the student glues the card onto his paper and uses the details to write a story problem. Then he solves the problem before repeating the activity with another card.

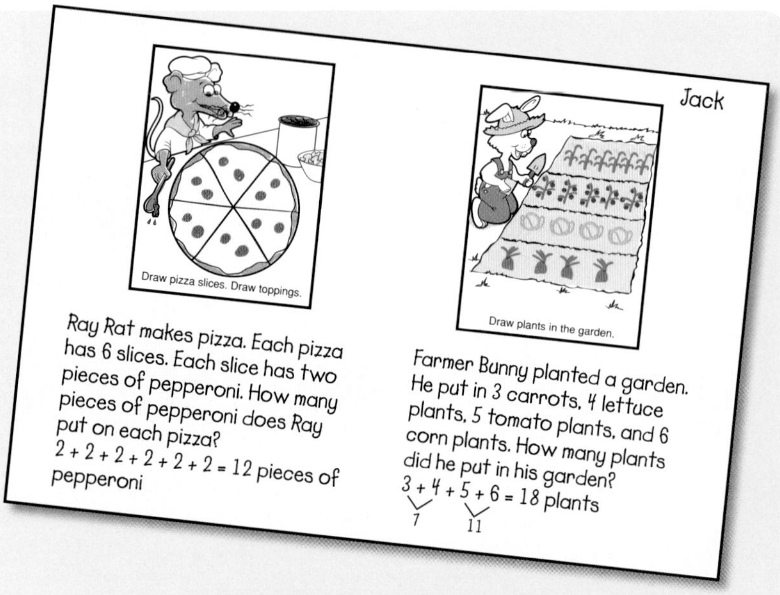

Centered on Probability

Probability

To set up these centers, make a class supply of the reproducible on page 46. Also gather the items listed below and place them at four different centers.

- Center 1: penny
- Center 2: die
- Center 3: three sets of five items that are the same shape and size, but different colors (for example, five green blocks, five red blocks, and five blue blocks)
- Center 4: a spinner divided into four sections, with each section having one of the following shapes inside: triangle, square, rectangle, and circle

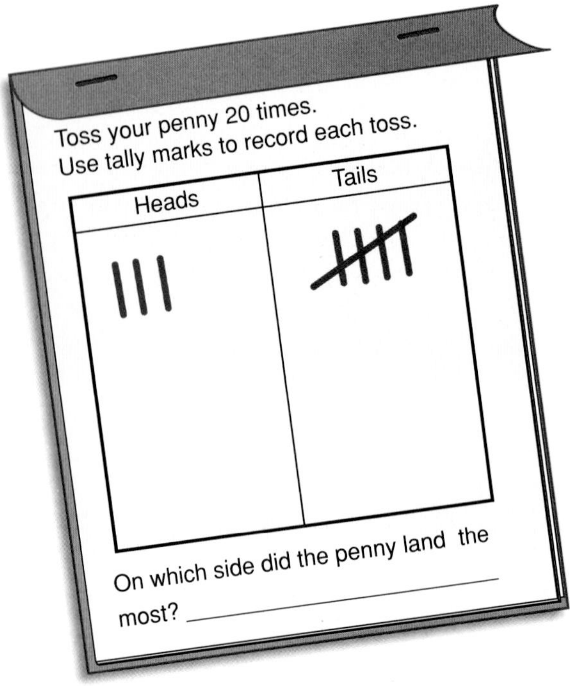

To start, give each child a copy of the reproducible. The student cuts apart the pages, stacks them, and staples them together between two construction paper covers. She visits each center and writes a prediction of the experiment's outcome on the back of the page. Then she uses the directions on the page to complete the experiment and record the results.

Jean Erickson
Grace Christian Academy
West Allis, WI

Math CENTERS

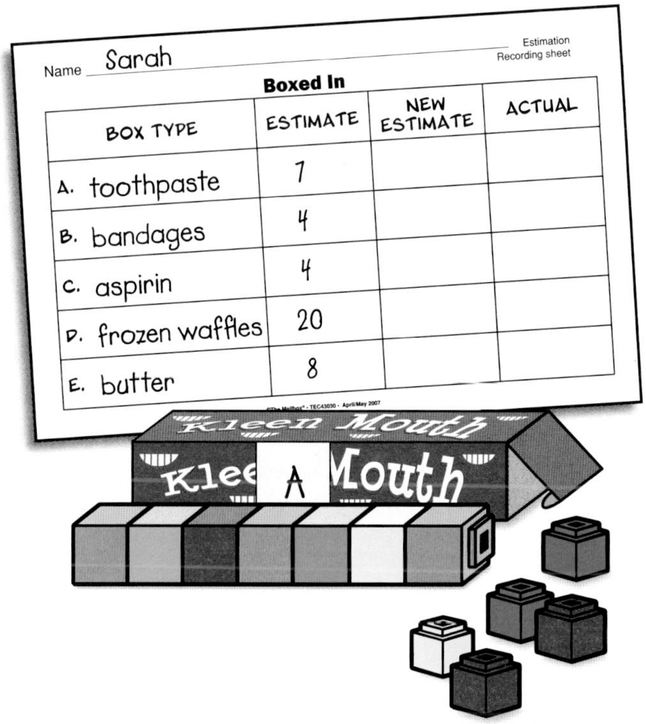

Name Sarah — Estimation Recording sheet

Boxed In

BOX TYPE	ESTIMATE	NEW ESTIMATE	ACTUAL
A. toothpaste	7		
B. bandages	4		
C. aspirin	4		
D. frozen waffles	20		
E. butter	8		

Boxed In

Estimation

Discarded household boxes and some linking cubes make this estimation activity a snap! In advance, collect five empty boxes of different sizes and write a letter on each one. If desired, also cut off one set of flaps from each box. Next, place a class supply of the recording sheet at the top of page 47 at a center with the boxes and a supply of Unifix cubes. A child records the box type next to each matching letter and records an estimate of how many cubes will fit inside for each. Then she stacks cubes inside the first box until she has filled half of it. Then she re-estimates the number of cubes needed and writes the new number. She continues adding cubes until she has filled the box and records the total used. She repeats the process with the remaining boxes.

Colleen Dabney
Williamsburg-JCC Schools
Williamsburg, VA

Weighing In

Using nonstandard units to measure weight

Make a class supply of the recording sheet at the bottom of page 47 and place the copies at a center with a balance scale and Unifix cubes. Also set out a variety of sets of objects, such as fish-shaped crackers, beans, craft sticks, or base-ten cubes. To complete the activity, a child refers to the table and places Unifix cubes in one bucket to equal the first animal's weight. Next, the student chooses a set of objects to compare with the animal's weight. He adds the objects to the other bucket until the scale balances. Then the child counts the objects, writes the number on his paper, and repeats the process for each of the remaining animals. As time allows, have the student complete another column on his chart and compare the animals' weights using a different set of objects.

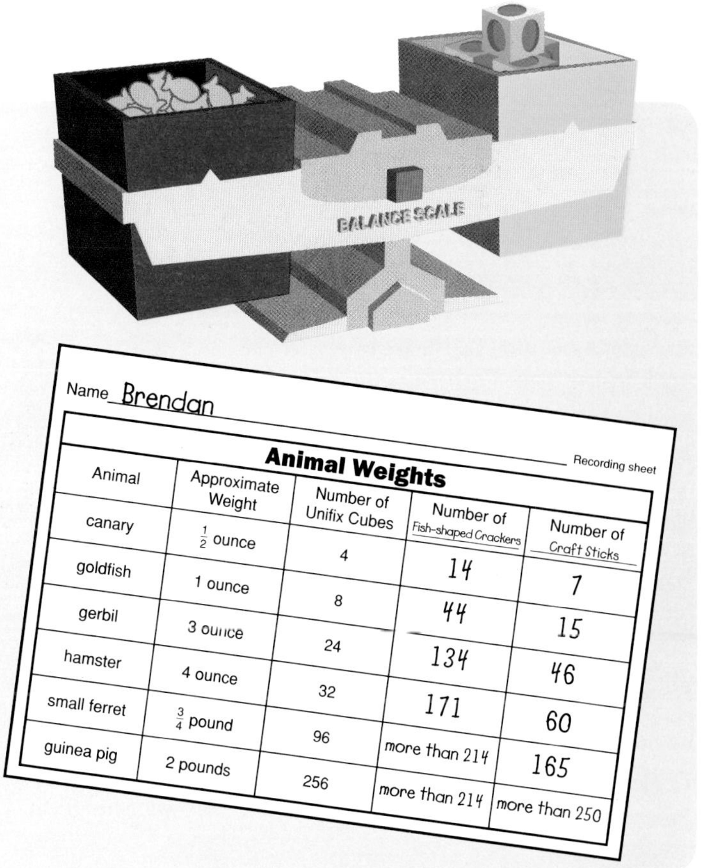

Name Brendan — Recording sheet

Animal Weights

Animal	Approximate Weight	Number of Unifix Cubes	Number of Fish-shaped Crackers	Number of Craft Sticks
canary	$\frac{1}{2}$ ounce	4	14	7
goldfish	1 ounce	8	44	15
gerbil	3 ounce	24	134	46
hamster	4 ounce	32	171	60
small ferret	$\frac{3}{4}$ pound	96	more than 214	165
guinea pig	2 pounds	256	more than 214	more than 250

Math CENTERS

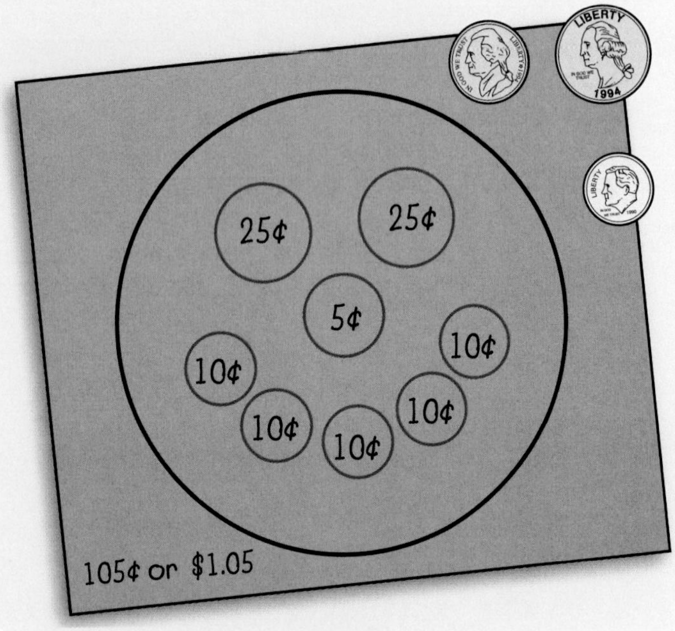

Value of a Picture

Coin values

All you need to total coin values at this simple center is a bag of plastic coins and a supply of paper. To complete the activity, a student arranges coins on her paper to make a desired picture. She traces around each coin, writes its value inside its corresponding circle, and then totals the values of all the coins.

Tracy Meabe
Crawford-Rodriguez Elementary
Jackson, NJ

May I Take Your Order, Please?

Adding money

At this center, pairs work together to practice adding money! Gather a variety of restaurant menus and place them at a center along with a supply of the order pad pattern on page 48. One child chooses a menu and names three or four things he would like to order. His partner writes down each item and uses the menu to find its price. Then he finds the total cost. Pairs take turns ordering and finding the total for as long as desired.

Gina Bittner
Hoff Elementary
Keenesburg, CO

Math CENTERS

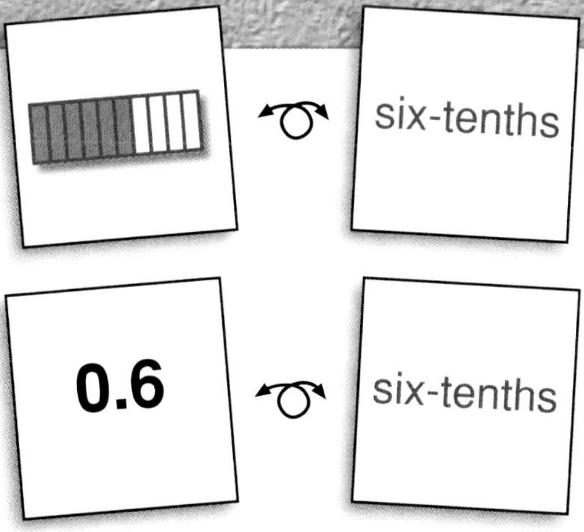

Meaningful Matches

Fractions and decimals

To prepare this ready-to-go center, cut out the fraction bar and decimal cards on page 41. Put the cards in a resealable plastic bag and place the bag at a center. A child removes the cards, placing them yellow side up. She matches each fraction bar to its decimal equivalent. When all matches have been made, she turns the cards over to check her work.

In View

Comparing fractions

Gather four or more interesting pictures and make a copy of each one. Trim each copy so it is the same size as the original. Cut the pictures from each pair into halves, thirds, fourths, or fifths (strips), making sure they represent two different fractions. Then write the fractional part on the back of each piece and label a resealable bag with a picture descriptor. Store both sets of picture pieces in the bag. To complete the activity, a child chooses a bag and removes the pieces. She arranges the pieces to make the two pictures side by side. The student turns over one strip on each picture, identifies the fractional parts, and writes a comparison statement. She continues by turning over one strip at a time and writes as many comparison statements as she can.

Carolyn M. Burant, St. John Vianney School, Brookfield, WI

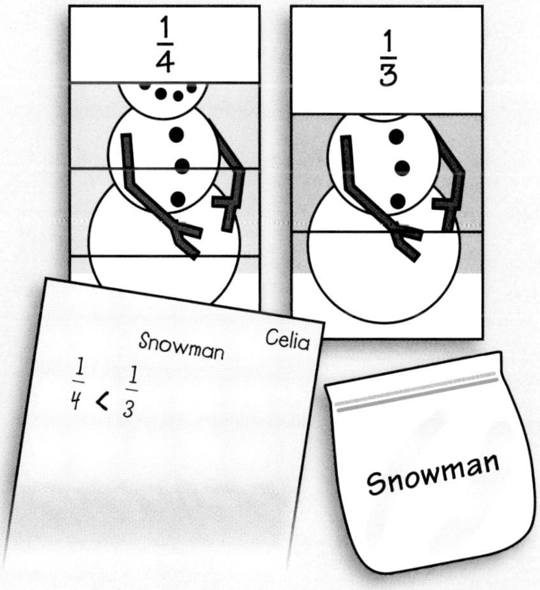

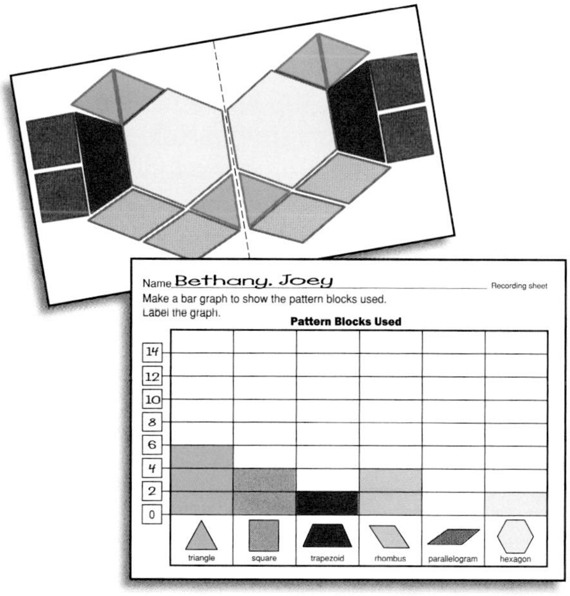

Pattern Block Symmetry

Symmetry

Combine symmetry and graphing in one easy-to-prepare partner center! Place pattern blocks, blank paper, and copies of the recording sheet on page 48 at a center. A student pair uses pattern blocks to create one symmetrical design on the blank paper. When completed, the students trace the blocks and color the resulting shapes. Then the duo labels and completes the graph to show the blocks used.

Alexandra Ballough, Yalesville Elementary, Yalesville, CT

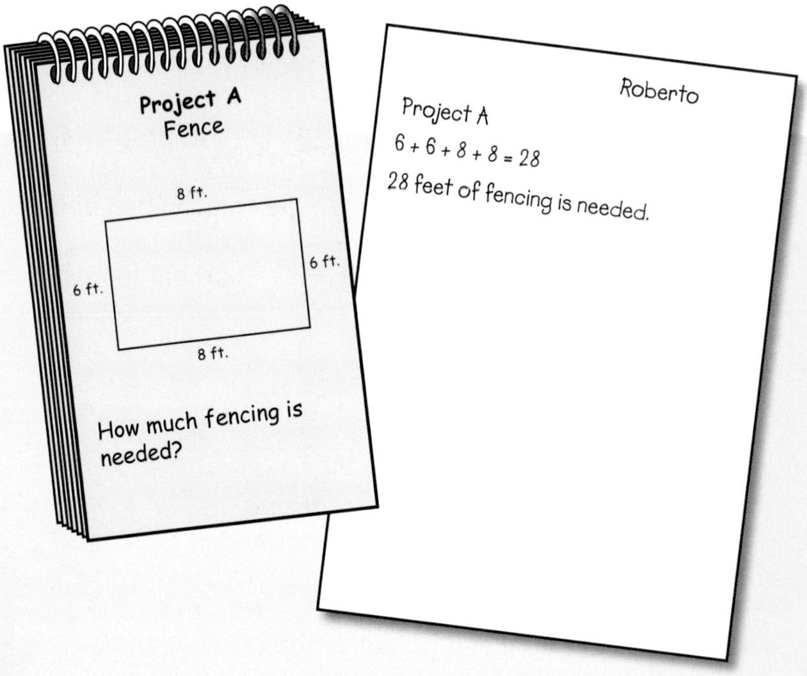

Larry Landscaper

Perimeter and area

Cut apart the notepad pages from a copy of page 49 and staple them in order. (To make the notepad more realistic, bind the pages with a plastic binding comb instead.) Place the pages and answer key from page 94 at a center. A child reviews the landscaper's notes and then, on a sheet of paper, solves each project. He then uses the answer key to check his work.

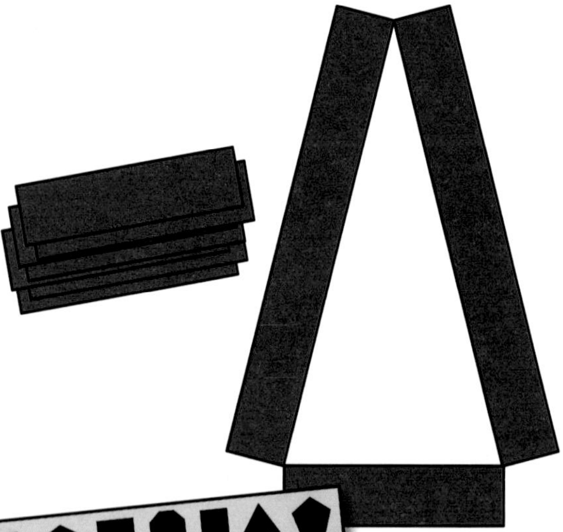

Building Buddies

Polygons

Partners use riddle clues to practice building polygons at this hands-on center. In advance, cut two 1" x 8" card stock strips and eight 1" x 4" strips. Place at a center the strips, a copy of the riddles and key on page 50, a math textbook or student dictionary, and paper. To start the activity, one child reads the first riddle aloud. Then she works with her partner to assemble the shape with the paper strips so that the interior lines of the strips form the sides of the polygon. If needed, the duo refers to the math book or dictionary to help identify the shape. Next, each child writes the riddle's number on her paper, draws the shape, and writes the shape's name. Students continue the activity until all the riddles are read and shapes are made.

Jean Erickson
Milwaukee, WI

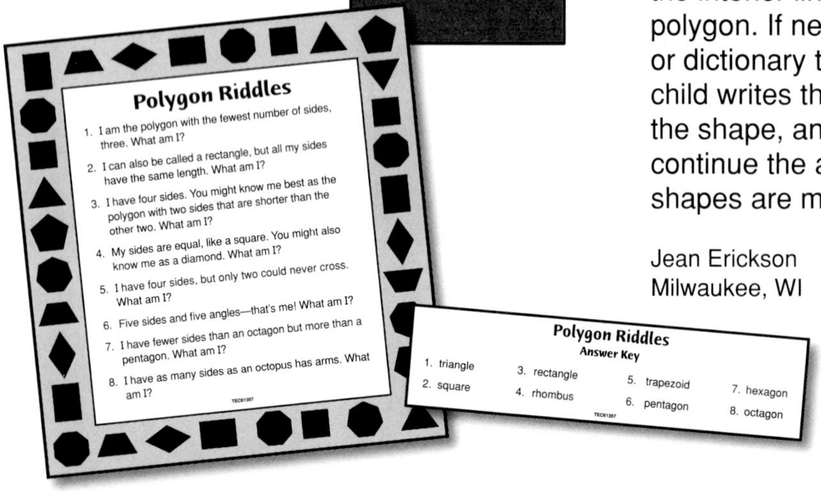
Polygon Riddles

1. I am the polygon with the fewest number of sides, three. What am I?
2. I can also be called a rectangle, but all my sides have the same length. What am I?
3. I have four sides. You might know me best as the polygon with two sides that are shorter than the other two. What am I?
4. My sides are equal, like a square. You might also know me as a diamond. What am I?
5. I have four sides, but only two could never cross. What am I?
6. Five sides and five angles—that's me! What am I?
7. I have fewer sides than an octagon but more than a pentagon. What am I?
8. I have as many sides as an octopus has arms. What am I?

TEC61357

Polygon Riddles
Answer Key

1. triangle
2. square
3. rectangle
4. rhombus
5. trapezoid
6. pentagon
7. hexagon
8. octagon

TEC61357

Colorful Counters

What You Need

division flash cards 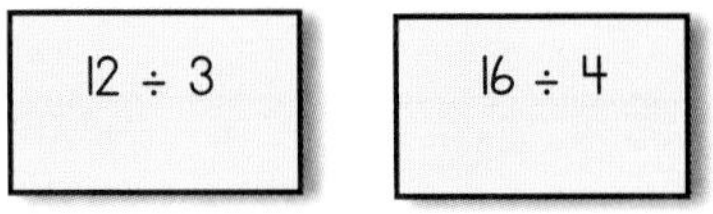

counters 

paper 

What You Do

1. Take a card and copy the problem. 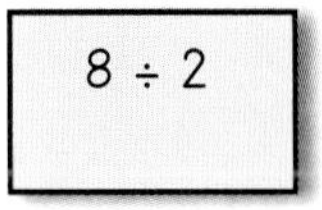

2. Use counters to show the dividend. 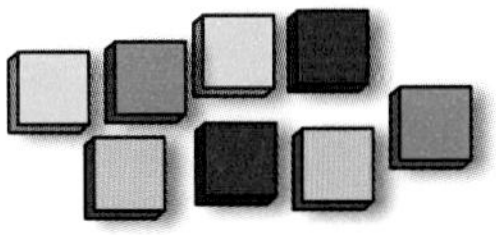

3. Divide the counters into sets to match the divisor. 

4. Count the counters in each set.

5. Write the quotient. 

6. Repeat Steps 1–5 nine more times.

Step-by-step center activity: Remove this activity card and put it in a plastic page protector for durability. Then put the activity card and the needed materials at a center.

Use with "Tools for Work" on page 31.

956	447	641	705
893	540	635	934
131	584	410	462
645	579	328	179
350	203	464	733
214	512	253	828
652	166	917	702
125	889	221	198
497	280	376	301

TEC61357	TEC61357	TEC61357

tens TEC61357	ones TEC61357	hundreds TEC61357	tens TEC61357
ones TEC61357	hundreds TEC61357	tens TEC61357	hundreds TEC61357
tens TEC61357	tens TEC61357	ones TEC61357	ones TEC61357
ones TEC61357	ones TEC61357	tens TEC61357	tens TEC61357
hundreds TEC61357	hundreds TEC61357	hundreds TEC61357	hundreds TEC61357
ones TEC61357	hundreds TEC61357	ones TEC61357	hundreds TEC61357
tens TEC61357	ones TEC61357	tens TEC61357	tens TEC61357
tens TEC61357	hundreds TEC61357	ones TEC61357	tens TEC61357
ones TEC61357	ones TEC61357	hundreds TEC61357	hundreds TEC61357

Use with "Meaningful Matches" on page 35.

	0.1		0.2
	0.3		0.4
	0.5	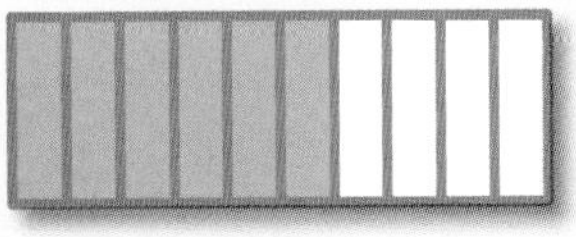	0.6
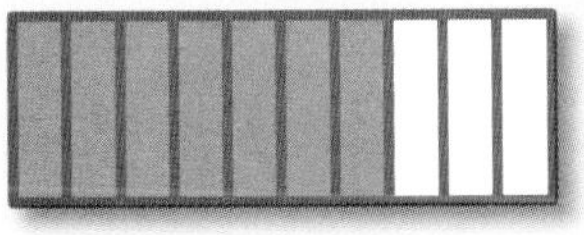	0.7	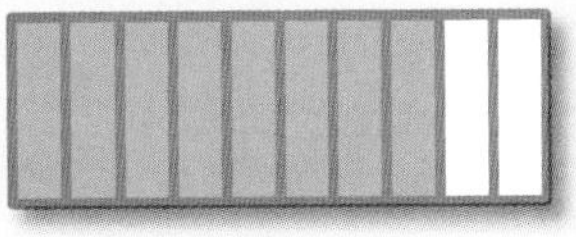	0.8
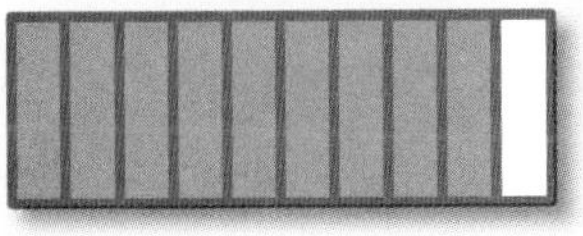	0.9	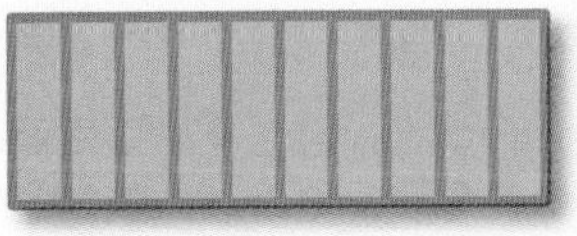	1.0

two-tenths TEC61357	two-tenths TEC61357	one-tenth TEC61357	one-tenth TEC61357
four-tenths TEC61357	four-tenths TEC61357	three-tenths TEC61357	three-tenths TEC61357
six-tenths TEC61357	six-tenths TEC61357	five-tenths TEC61357	five-tenths TEC61357
eight-tenths TEC61357	eight-tenths TEC61357	seven-tenths TEC61357	seven-tenths TEC61357
ten-tenths TEC61357	ten-tenths TEC61357	nine-tenths TEC61357	nine-tenths TEC61357

Use with "Number Jewels" on page 28.

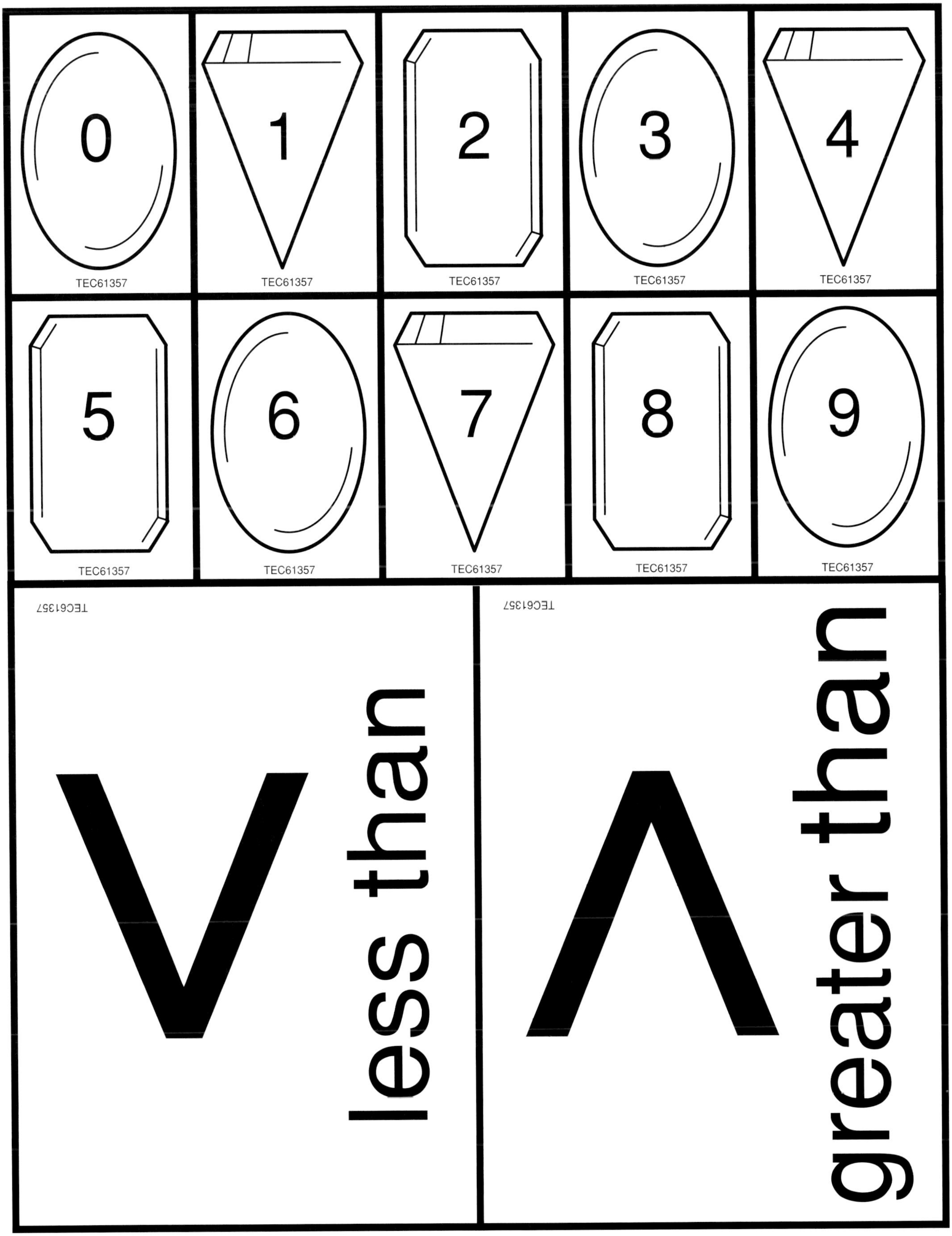

Sun Cards

Use with “Sunny Facts” on page 30.

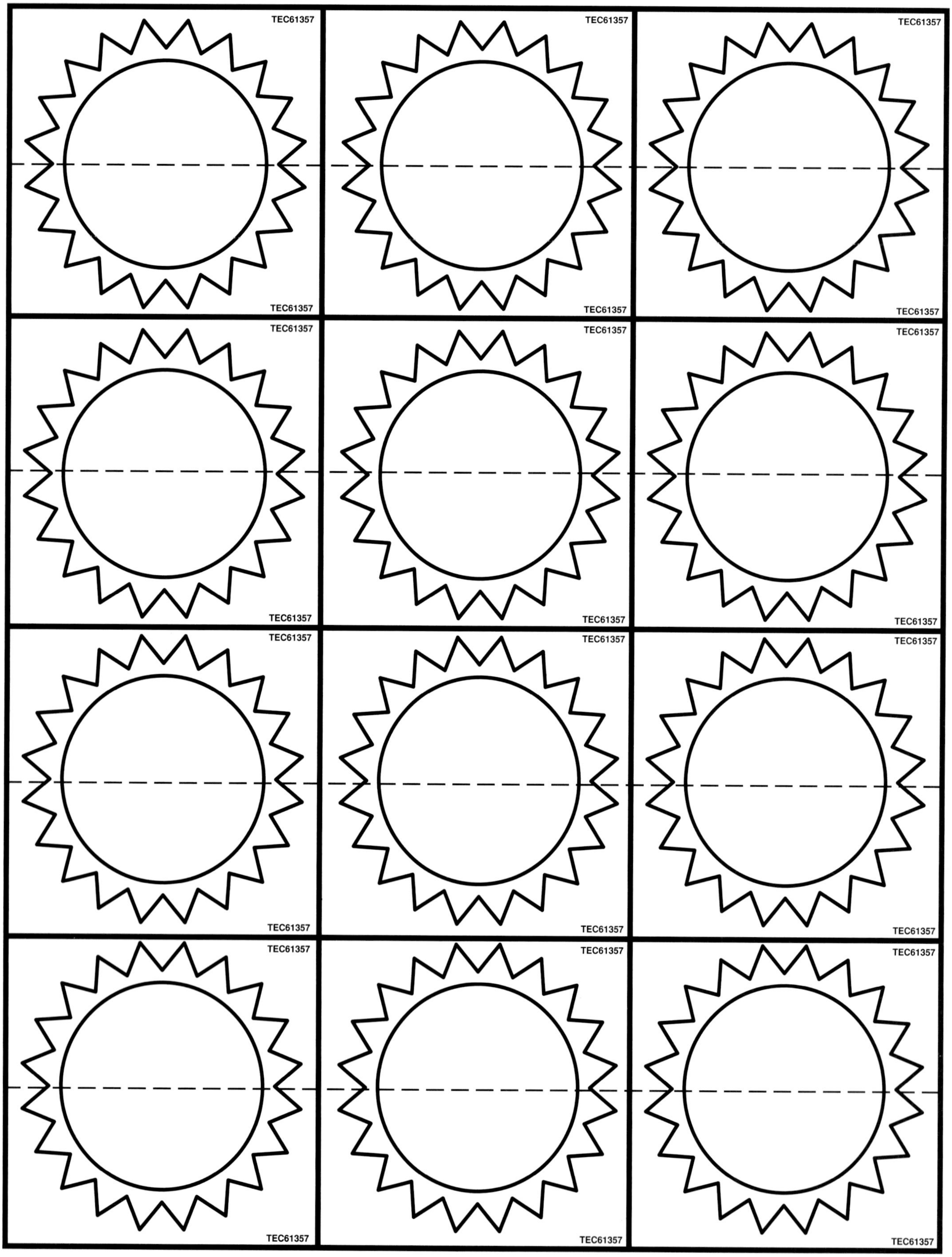

Use with "Story Problem Scenes" on page 32.

Draw pizza slices. Draw toppings.

TEC61357

Draw pictures in the boxes.

TEC61357

Draw fish.

TEC61357

Draw plants in the garden.

TEC61357

Recording Booklet

Use with "Centered on Probability" on page 32.

Toss your penny 20 times.
Use tally marks to record each toss.

Heads	Tails

On which side did the penny land the most? ____________________

TEC61357

Roll the die 20 times.
Draw an X in the matching box each time.

1	2	3	4	5	6

Which number was rolled the most?

______

TEC61357

Draw an item from the bag.
Color a circle in the matching row.
Return the item to the bag.
Repeat until you have colored 20 circles.

Red	○ ○ ○ ○ ○ ○ ○ ○ ○ ○ ○ ○
Blue	○ ○ ○ ○ ○ ○ ○ ○ ○ ○ ○ ○
Green	○ ○ ○ ○ ○ ○ ○ ○ ○ ○ ○ ○

Which color was drawn the most?

____

TEC61357

Spin the spinner 20 times.
Use a tally mark to record each spin.

△	
□	
▭	
○	

Which shape was spun the most?

____

TEC61357

Name ______________________________

Boxed In

BOX TYPE	ESTIMATE	NEW ESTIMATE	ACTUAL
A.			
B.			
C.			
D.			
E.			

Name ______________________________

Animal Weights

Animal	Approximate Weight	Number of Unifix Cubes	Number of ________	Number of ________
canary	$\frac{1}{2}$ ounce	4		
goldfish	1 ounce	8		
gerbil	3 ounce	24		
hamster	4 ounce	32		
small ferret	$\frac{3}{4}$ pound	96		
guinea pig	2 pounds	256		

Note to the teacher: Use "Boxed In" with "Boxed In" on page 33. Use "Animal Weights" with "Weighing In" on page 33.

Order Pad Pattern

Use with "May I Take Your Order, Please?" on page 34.

Item	Price
	$ __ __ . __ __
	$ __ __ . __ __
	$ __ __ . __ __
	$ __ __ . __ __
	$ __ __ . __ __
	$ __ __ . __ __
Total:	$ __ __ . __ __

TEC61357

Name______________________________ Recording sheet

Make a bar graph to show the pattern blocks used.
Label the graph.

Pattern Blocks Used

	triangle	square	trapezoid	rhombus	parallelogram	hexagon
☐						
☐						
☐						
☐						
☐						
☐						
☐						
0						

 Note to the teacher: Use with "Pattern Block Symmetry" on page 35.

Use with "Larry Landscaper" on page 36.

Notes

Larry Landscaper

TEC61357

Fence Projects

Find the distance around the yard.

perimeter = $\ell + \ell + w + w$

Sod Projects

Find out how much grass is needed to cover the yard.

area = $\ell \times w$

Project A

Fence

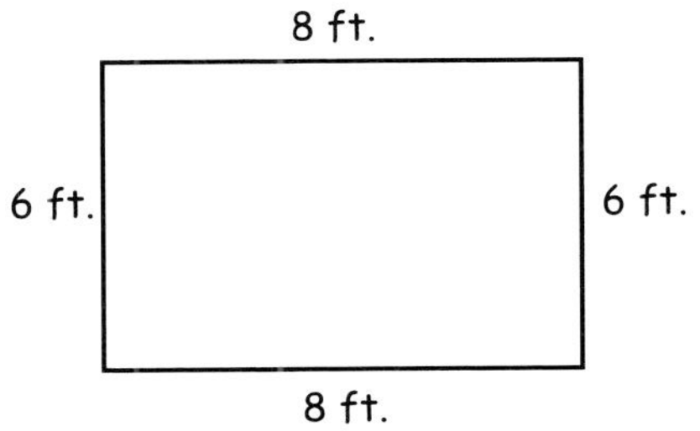

How much fencing is needed?

Project B

Fence

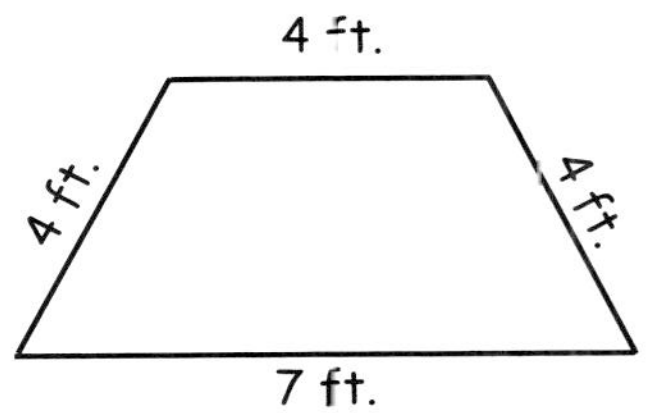

How much fencing is needed?

Project C

Sod

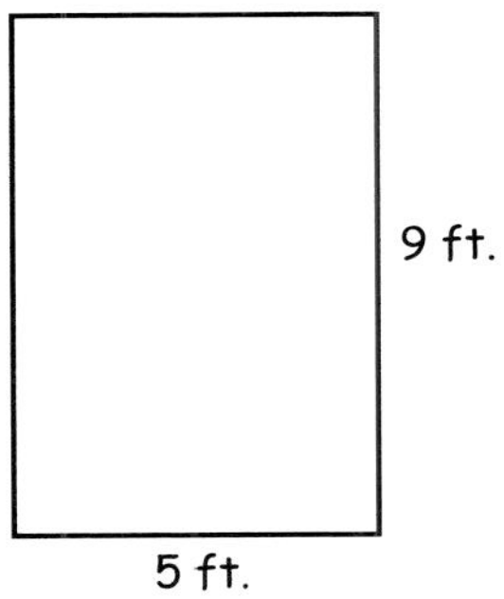

How much sod is needed?

Project D

Sod

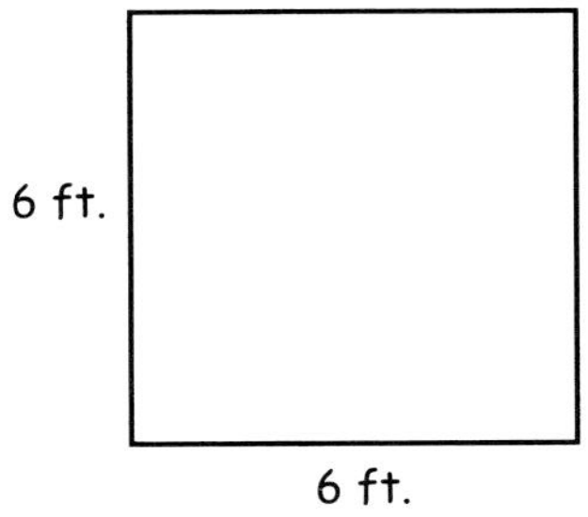

How much sod is needed?

Project E

Fence

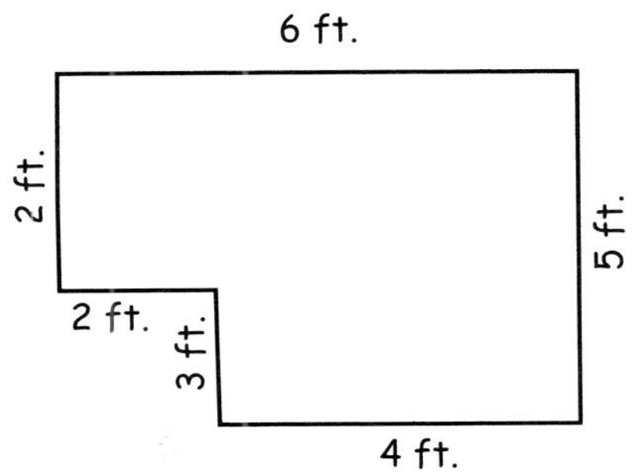

How much fencing is needed?

Project F

Sod

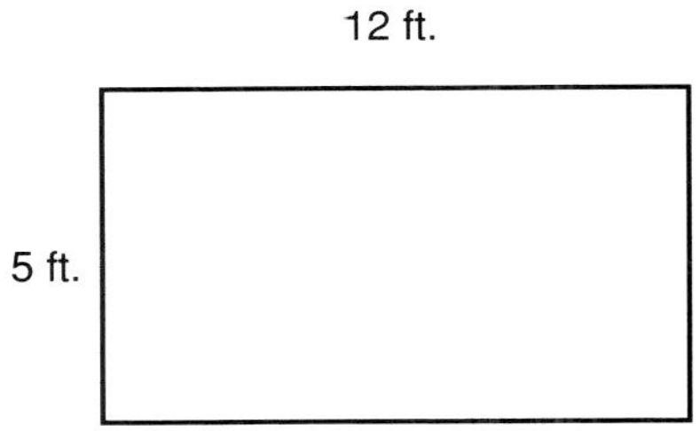

How much sod is needed?

Language Arts GAMES

Tic-Tac-Toe Times Four

Writing blends, digraphs, and vowel pairs

This fun game has the whole class working in pairs. To prepare, have each duo fold a sheet of construction paper in fourths, unfold it, and then draw a tic-tac-toe grid in each section. Also give each pair a mini whiteboard and a dry-erase marker. To play, call out the sound of a blend, digraph, or vowel combination in a whole word, using an instruction such as "Show the /er/ sound in *teacher*." Have Player 1 write the letters that make the sound in that word on the mini whiteboard; then announce the correct answer. Have Player 2 check the answer for correctness. If the answer is correct, Player 1 puts an X on the first grid. If incorrect, he does not make a mark. Player 2 then takes a turn in a similar manner, drawing an O on the grid if she is correct, and the game continues until tic-tac-toe is achieved or all the spaces on the grid are filled and the game ends in a tie. When one game has ended, the student pair starts a new game on another grid. Continue play in this manner until a duo completes all four grids or time is called.

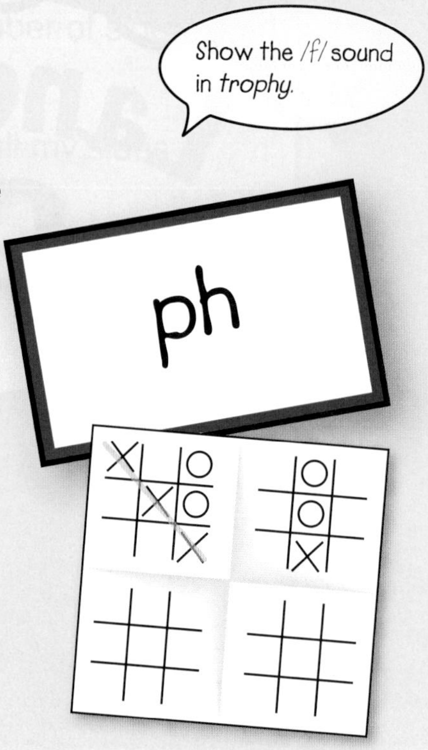

Adrienne Ambrose, Ormond Beach Elementary, Ormond Beach, FL

Undercover Sounds

Using blends and word families

To prepare this whole-class game, copy the grid on page 67. Program each of eight squares with a different blend and each of the other eight squares with a different word family that makes a word with at least one of the blends. Display the grid on the board and cover each grid square with a small sticky note.

To play, divide the class into teams and call on a team to choose two grid squares. Reveal the word parts on those two squares. If the team uses the two parts to make a word, shade in each corresponding gas gauge (to show that the word part cannot be reused) and write the word under the team's name on the board. If the two parts do not make a word, re-cover the spaces with the sticky notes. Continue until all spaces are revealed or no more words can be made. The team with the most words listed wins.

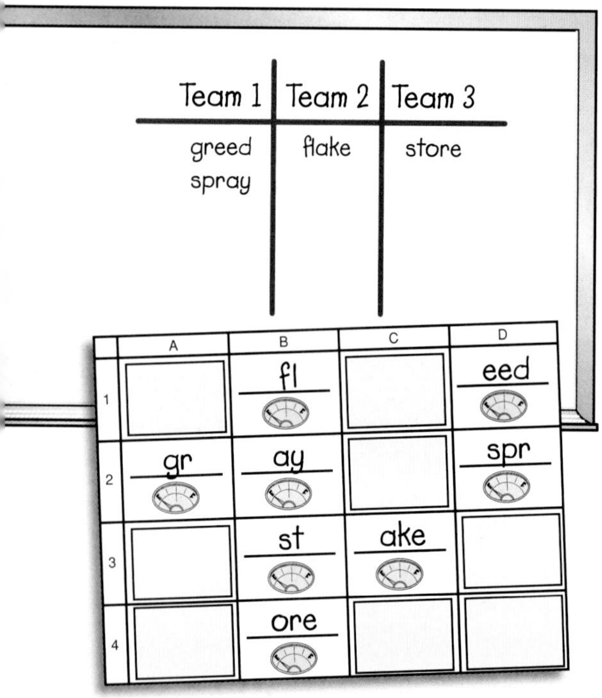

Molly Alvine, Van Allen Elementary, Mount Pleasant, IA

Moving Along

Word skills review

This variation on the Around the World game helps students review word skills. In advance, program a word or word part on each of a supply of index cards. To play, have one student stand near another student; then flash a card. The first of the two students to correctly read the word or word part advances, moving to stand near the next child on her right. Continue play in this manner as time allows.

Cora Boyer
Hunters Creek Elementary
Jacksonville, NC

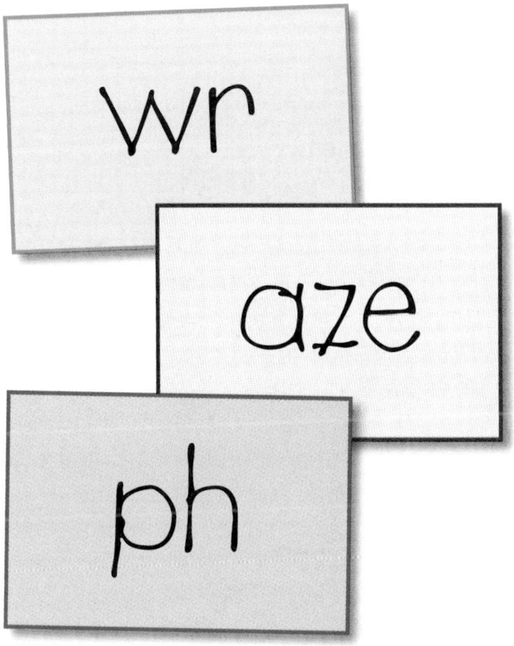

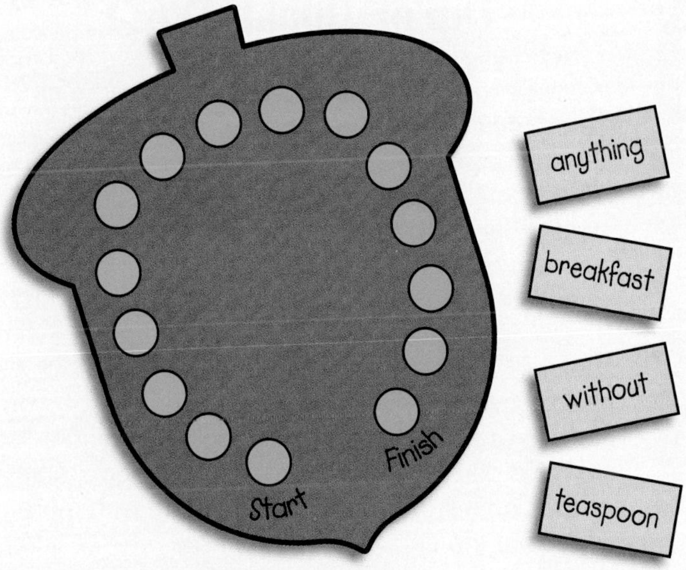

Around the Board

Spelling

In advance, make a gameboard by cutting a large seasonal shape out of poster board. Use adhesive dots to make a simple path around the border of the cutout and then label one dot "Start" and another "Finish" as shown. Program a supply of cards with different spelling words. To play, Player 1 draws a card and reads the word aloud. Player 2 spells the word. Player 1 checks the spelling and, if the word is spelled correctly, Player 2 moves her game marker ahead one space. If the word is spelled incorrectly, Player 2 remains in place. Players continue taking turns until one player reaches the finish space and wins the game.

Debbie Berris
Poinciana Day School
West Palm Beach, FL

Bang, Bam, Boom!

Word recognition

Here's a game that will surely generate an explosion of interest! Program a supply of cards with high-frequency or vocabulary words. Also program three distracter cards "Bang!" "Bam!" and "Boom!" Place the cards in a bag. To play, a student pulls a card from the bag, reads it aloud, and shows it to the other players. If she correctly reads the word, she keeps the card. If she misreads the word, she returns the card to the bag. If she chooses a distracter card, she returns it and all her accumulated cards to the bag. Players continue to take turns for a predetermined amount of time. The child with the most cards wins.

Gina Livingston
Southern Tier Catholic School
Olean, NY

Dip or Double Dip?

Inflectional endings

Divide the class into two teams and draw an ice cream cone on the board for each team. In turn, ask a student from each team to spell a word from the list shown. Direct the student to identify the word as either a dip word, a word whose final consonant is not doubled before an inflectional ending, or a double-dip word, a word whose final consonant is doubled. Then have him spell the word. If the student spells a dip word correctly, have him draw one ice cream scoop on his team's cone. If the student spells a double-dip word correctly, have him draw two ice cream scoops on his team's cone. The team with more scoops at the end of the game wins.

Laura Johnson
South Decatur Elementary
Greenburg, IN

Punctuation Cards

Recognizing appropriate inflection

To prepare this partner game, label a supply of index cards with sentences, questions, and exclamations, writing each one on a separate card. Also label three additional cards with a period, a question mark, and an exclamation point. To play the game, give one child the sentence cards and the other partner the punctuation cards. Player 1 reads a sentence aloud with the correct inflection. Player 2 holds up the matching punctuation card, based on the inflection he heard. Play continues with players periodically switching roles.

Jennifer Kohnke
Nature Ridge Elementary, Bartlett, IL,

Stacie Wright
Millington School, Millington, NJ

Punctuation Police

Identifying correct punctuation

Have each child write a different sentence on each of two sentence strips—one sentence with correct punctuation and another with incorrect punctuation. Put students in teams and have each team sort its sentence strips into two piles: correct and incorrect. Next, choose two students from one team to serve as the punctuation police and have them step outside the classroom. While the pair is out of the room, choose one group to place an incorrect sentence in a pocket chart. Have each of the other groups place one of its correct strips in the chart. Then invite the police back into the room. Challenge the pair to determine which sentence has incorrect punctuation. If the pair is correct, the students earn a point for their team. Continue playing in a similar manner, choosing pairs of students from different groups to serve as the police.

adapted from an idea by Jolyn Haye
Peach Hill Academy
Moorpark, CA

Catch of the Day

Capitalization rules

To prepare this partner game, program two sets of index cards: one with capitalized words and the other with matching rules. Put each set of cards in a plastic bucket and place the buckets at a center. Player 1 chooses a card from each bucket. He shows the word card to his partner and then reads the rule aloud. If the rule card matches the word card, he keeps the pair and takes another turn. If the rule and word cards don't match, he returns them to the buckets. The player with more pairs wins.

Melinda Smith
Cypress Ridge Elementary
Clermont, FL

Name That Word

Compound words

For this partner activity, cut out a copy of the game and answer key cards on page 68. Have one player shuffle the definition cards and stack the cards facedown while the other player arranges the word cards faceup. To begin, Player 1 draws a definition card and reads it aloud. She chooses two word cards to make a compound word that matches the definition. Player 2 checks the answer key. If the answer is correct, Player 1 keeps the three cards and her turn ends. If it is not correct, she returns the cards. Then Player 2 takes a turn. The game continues until all cards have been matched. The player with more cards wins.

Laura Johnson
South Decatur Elementary
Greensburg, IN

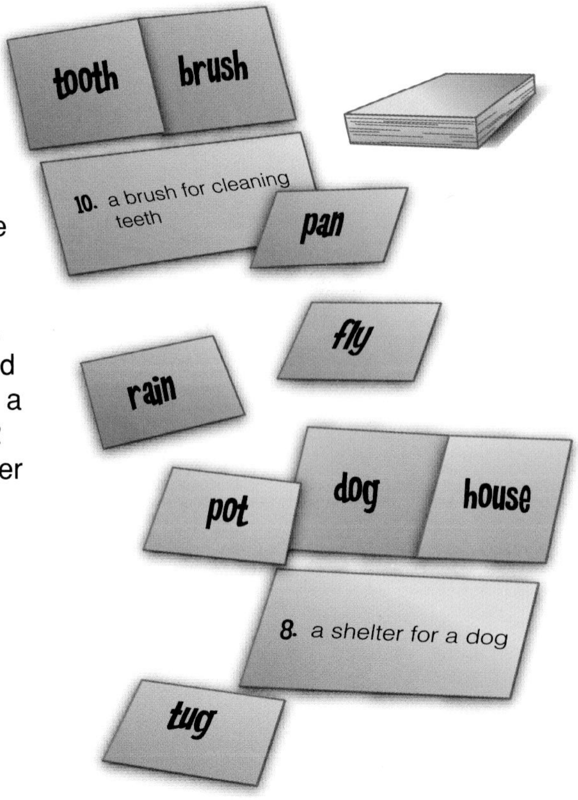

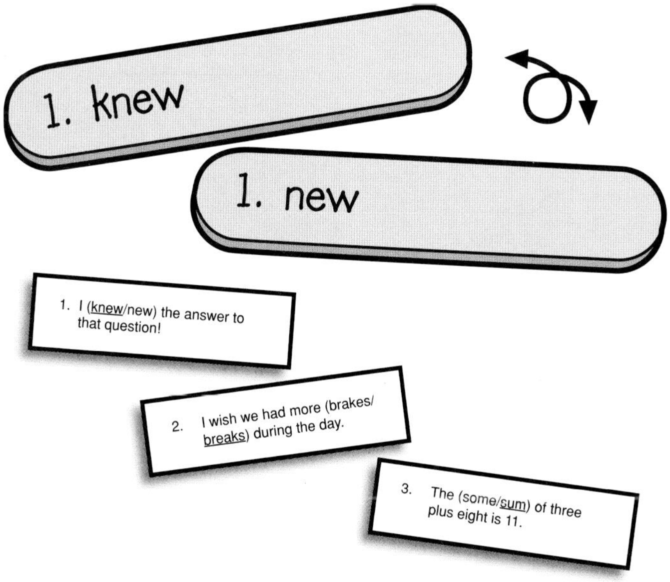

Stick With It
Homophones

To prepare this partner game, copy the homophone sentence cards on page 69. Also program each side of a jumbo craft stick with a sentence number and one of the matching homophones from the pair listed. Place the sticks and the sentences at a center. A student reads a number and his partner locates the matching stick. Then the child reads the corresponding sentence and his partner displays the side of the stick with the matching homophone. After five sentences have been read, the students switch roles and continue with the activity.

Jennifer Winkelman
Tebbetts, MO

See page 61 for a two-player SYNONYM game!

Quick Thinking
Using prefixes and suffixes

To prepare for this small-group game, gather four different-colored sheets of construction paper. Write a different prefix or suffix at the top of each sheet. Designate four stations in the classroom and place one of the papers at each station along with a pencil. Divide students into four groups, and have each group assemble at a different station. At your signal, invite the groups to list on the paper words containing the corresponding prefix or suffix. After a short amount of time, have the groups stop and rotate to the next station. Continue in this manner until each group has visited each station.

Language Arts GAMES

Sentence Sense

Creating sentences with meaning

Before the game, create a word bank for each of the following parts of speech: nouns, verbs, and adjectives. Write each word bank on a separate sheet of chart paper and in a different color. Post the lists in the classroom. Begin the activity by dividing students into groups of three or four. Instruct each group to choose two nouns, one verb, and one adjective from the list. Then have the group write a sentence that includes the chosen words. Remind groups that their sentences may be silly, but they must have meaning. Continue having students write sentences in this manner for as long as desired.

David Green
North Shore Country Day School
Winnetka, IL

See page 63 for a partner game that reinforces PLURAL NOUNS!

Pronto!

Common and proper nouns

holiday Thanksgiving Day Halloween	**cereal** Frosted Puffs	**month** October May June
restaurant McBurger	**teacher** Ms. Davis	**planet** Mars
author Kevin Henkes	**state** New York	**day** Sunday

This fast-paced game will have students wanting more! To prepare, make a nine-space grid as shown. Program each space with a common noun. (If desired, make four different versions of the grid to ensure different student outcomes.) Organize students into small groups and give each child a grid. Then have students fill in as many spaces as possible with corresponding proper nouns. After a predetermined amount of time, signal students to stop writing. Have each child pass her grid to the classmate on her left. Continue in this manner until each child has written on all the grids. Finally, challenge each student to write a paragraph using as many of the proper nouns on her grid as possible.

Stacie Stone Davis
Lima, NY

Verb Lotto

Adding -s and -es to present-tense verbs, subject-verb agreement

This whole-class game combines fun and practice! To prepare, display on the board the sentences shown; then cover them from students' view. Have each child fold a sheet of paper in half four times, creasing each fold line. Next, he unfolds the paper and labels each space with "s" or "es" as desired. To begin the game, designate a method to determine the winner (four in a row, four corners, etc.). Then reveal a sentence. Each student decides whether *-s* or *-es* should be added to the underlined word to make it correct, and then he writes the word in a corresponding space. Play continues in this manner until a student calls out, "Lotto!"

Stacie Stone Davis
Lima, NY

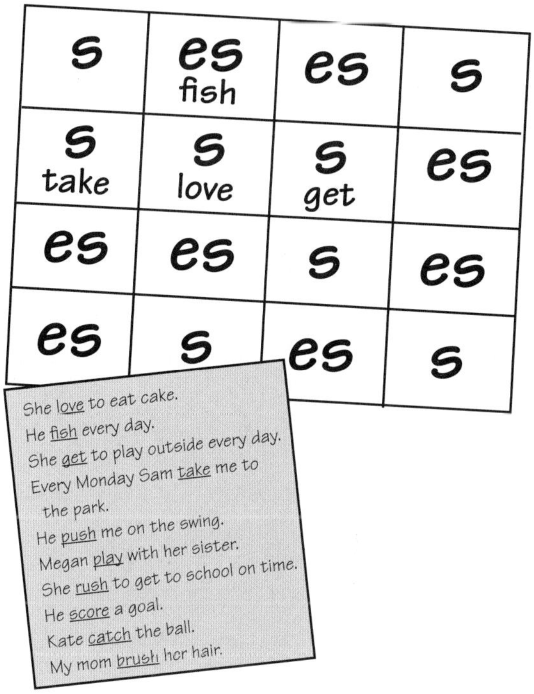

Action-Packed Games

Verb tenses

With minimal preparation, this trio of games provides a quick grammar review. Have each small group review and cut apart a copy of page 70. Direct students to set the "Kaboom!" cards aside and then shuffle the remaining cards. Guide students to play one of the games described below.

Speed Sort: On your signal, have each group organize its cards according to tense. The first team to correctly sort its cards wins.

Prove It: Use one of the verbs from the cards in a sentence. The first student from any team to raise her hand, name the verb tense, and then show the matching card as proof that her response is correct earns a point. The team with the most points wins.

Kaboom! Direct students to place all their cards, including the "Kaboom!" cards, in a paper bag. In turn, have a student from each team take a card from the bag and read it aloud. If the card is a word card, the child names the verb's other two tenses. If correct, she keeps the card for her team; if incorrect, she returns it to the bag. If a "Kaboom!" card is drawn, she returns all the cards collected by her team.

Barclay Marcell
Roosevelt School
Park Ridge, IL

Language Arts GAMES

Important Ingredients

Story elements

For this partner game, make two copies of the gameboard from the top of page 71 and one copy of the game cards at the bottom of the same page. Cut apart the game cards, program the back of each one with the corresponding story element (or provide students with the answer key from page 95), and stack them faceup. To play, Player 1 draws a card, reads it aloud, and names the corresponding story element. Then he turns the card over to check his answer (or checks the answer key). If correct, Player 1 places a marker, such as dried pasta, on the corresponding pot and keeps the card. If incorrect, he returns the card to the bottom of the stack. Player 2 takes a turn in the same manner, and play continues until all cards have been read. The player with more markers wins.

Sheila Ziegler, Red Rock Elementary, Mattawa, WA

! See page 65 for a two-player game about FORMS OF LITERATURE!

Blast Off

Recognizing reference materials and their parts

For this partner game, have each player label a rocket on a copy of page 69 with his name. Next, direct each pair to cut apart the game cards from a copy of page 72, shuffle the cards, and stack them facedown. To play, Player 1 takes the top card and reads aloud the clues. He locates the term that matches the clues, colors the space on his rocket, and returns the card to the bottom of the stack. If the term is already colored on his rocket, he returns the card to the bottom of the stack. Then Player 2 takes a turn in the same manner. The first player to color all eight sections of his rocket wins. Have students use a copy of the answer key from page 95 to check their answers.

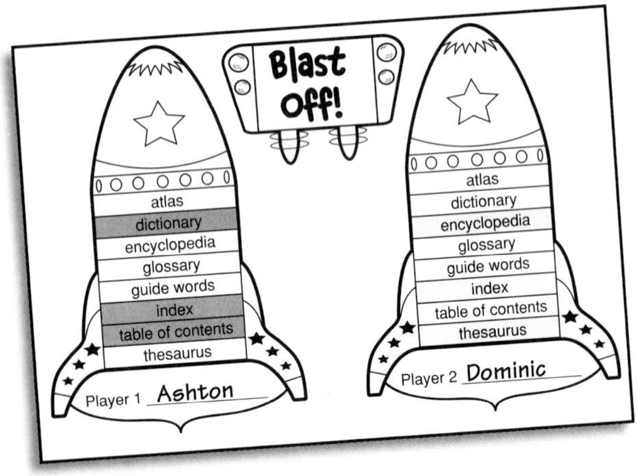

Jean Erickson, Grace Christian Academy, West Allis, WI

A Place to Call Home

Synonyms

Directions for two players:

1. Put a game marker on the first space.
2. When it is your turn, read the words on the space. Tell your partner the two words that have the same meaning.
3. Have your partner check the answer key. If you are correct, move ahead one space. If you are incorrect, stay put.
4. Take turns in this manner. The first player to reach the gingerbread house wins.

Player 1

1. woman — lady, man
2. slow — speedy, poky
3. run — stroll, jog
4. little — small, long
5. sly — sneaky, honest
6. old — young, aged
7. chase — follow, lead
8. wet — dry, soaked
9. toss — throw, hold

Player 2

1. brave — fearless, chicken
2. catch — trap, miss
3. late — early, overdue
4. real — fake, true
5. cottage — house, school
6. shout — yell, whisper
7. fast — slow, quick
8. tired — worn-out, active
9. snout — nose, tail

The Best of The Mailbox® *Centers & Games* • ©The Mailbox® Books • TEC61357 • Key p. 94

Partner Game: Mount the gameboard on construction paper. Provide a twosome with the gameboard, two game markers, and a copy of the keys from page 94.

To the Lemonade Stand!

Plural Nouns

START

1 lemons / lemones

2 teeth / tooths

3 kisss / kisses

4 beachs / beaches

5 hills / hilles

6 mice / mouses

7 feet / feets

8 berrys / berries

9 mans / men

10 bushs / bushes

11 geese / gooses

12 ladys / ladies

13 childs / children

14 ponys / ponies

15 women / womans

16 bunchs / bunches

17 parties / partys

18 boxs / boxes

19 boys / boies

20 mixs / mixes

Finish

Directions for two players:

1. Put your markers on START.
2. When it's your turn, roll a die and move your marker.
3. Read the words. Spell the correct plural word aloud while your partner checks the answer key. If correct, leave your marker. If incorrect, move your marker back one space.
4. The first player to reach FINISH wins.

Partner Game: Make a copy of the answer key on page 94. Place the key with this gameboard, two game markers, and a die.

Flipping for Stories

Directions:

1. Shuffle the game cards. Place them facedown as you would to play Concentration.
2. When it's your turn, flip over two cards.
   If you have a word card *(mystery, fantasy, biography)* and a matching description card, keep the cards.
   If not, turn the cards facedown.
3. The player with more card pairs wins.

mystery	fantasy	biography
1. This is a type of fiction.	2. This is a type of fiction.	3. This is a type of nonfiction.
mystery	fantasy	biography
4. The main character is a detective or investigator.	5. The main character could not exist in real life.	6. It tells about a real person's life events.
mystery	fantasy	biography
7. A crime or puzzle needs to be solved.	8. Characters may include talking animals. Characters may have magical powers.	9. Photos or maps are often shown. Direct quotes may be used.
mystery	fantasy	biography
10. Clues help the main character and the reader solve the problem.	11. The setting is a make-believe place.	12. This tells how the person did or did not make the world a better place.

Partner game: Cut out the direction and game cards. Give a pair of students the cards and a copy of the answer key on page 95.

	A	B	C	D
1	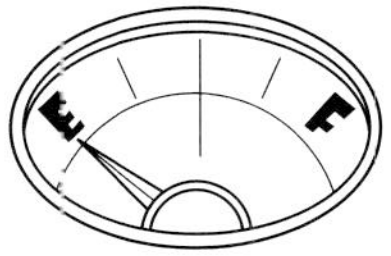	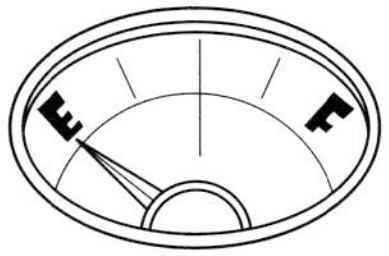	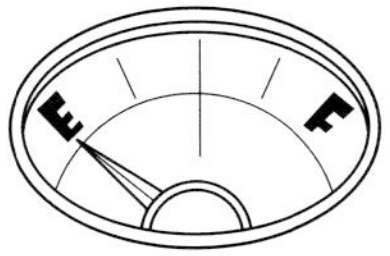	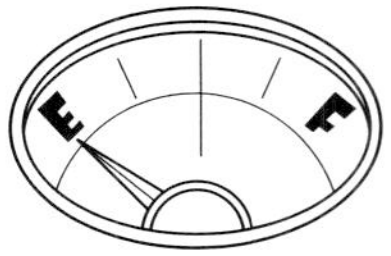
2	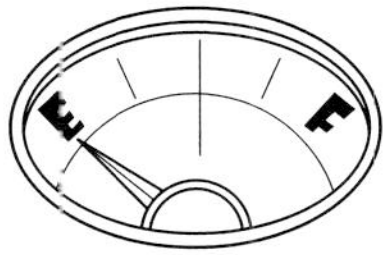	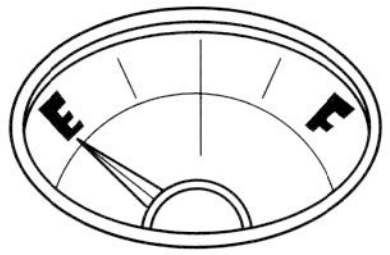	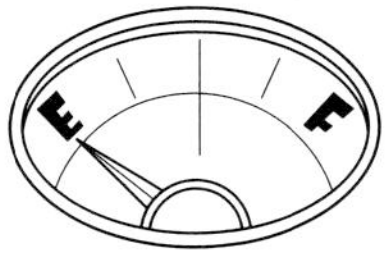	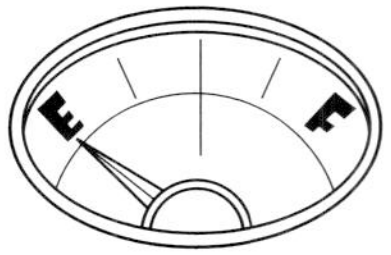
3	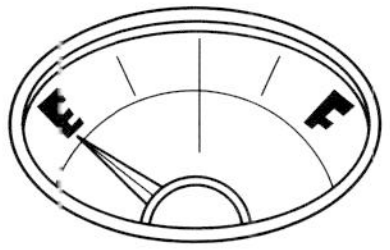	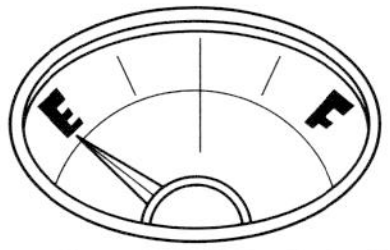	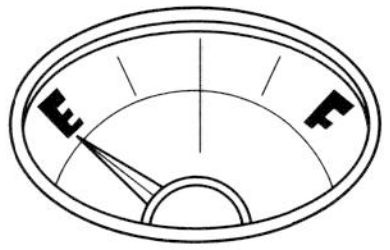	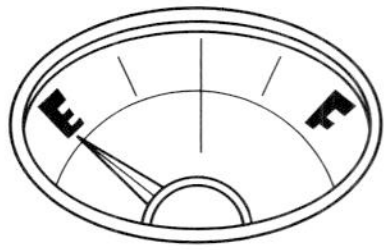
4	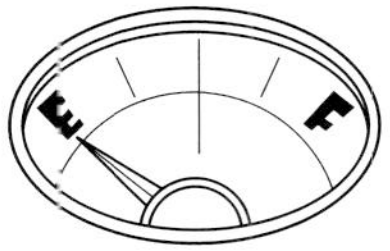	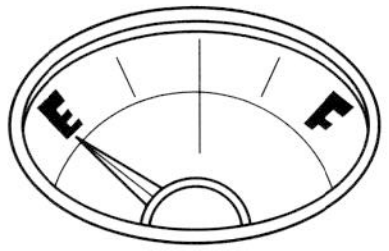	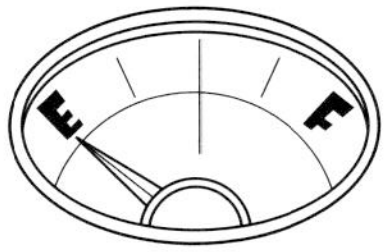	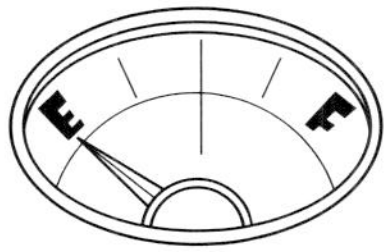

Note to the teacher: Use with “Undercover Sounds” on page 52.

Game and Answer Key Cards

Use with “Name That Word” on page 56.

1. a button found at an outside door that is pushed to ring a bell TEC61357	**2.** a poisonous snake with a rattle at the end of its tail TEC61357	**3.** an arc of colors that appears in the sky TEC61357
4. a flying insect with large, brightly colored wings TEC61357	**5.** the nail of a finger TEC61357	**6.** a pot in which to grow plants TEC61357
7. a sea creature that has five arms TEC61357	**8.** a shelter for a dog TEC61357	**9.** a flat cake made of batter and cooked in a pan TEC61357
10. a brush for cleaning teeth TEC61357	**11.** a fire built outdoors, such as at a camp TEC61357	**12.** a U-shaped band of iron that is fitted to a horse’s hoof TEC61357
13. a powerful boat used for towing or pushing TEC61357	**14.** a piece of land used by children for playing TEC61357	**15.** a box that contains sand for children to play in TEC61357

pan TEC61357	flower TEC61357	rain TEC61357	rattle TEC61357	star TEC61357	play TEC61357
camp TEC61357	butter TEC61357	tooth TEC61357	dog TEC61357	finger TEC61357	door TEC61357
horse TEC61357	tug TEC61357	sand TEC61357	ground TEC61357	shoe TEC61357	fire TEC61357
snake TEC61357	nail TEC61357	pot TEC61357	bell TEC61357	bow TEC61357	house TEC61357
cake TEC61357	fly TEC61357	sea TEC61357	brush TEC61357	box TEC61357	boat TEC61357

Answer Key

1. doorbell
2. rattlesnake
3. rainbow
4. butterfly
5. fingernail
6. flowerpot
7. seastar
8. doghouse
9. pancake
10. toothbrush
11. campfire
12. horseshoe
13. tugboat
14. playground
15. sandbox

TEC61357

Use with "Stick With It" on page 57.

1. I (knew/new) the answer to that question! TEC61357	6. Saturday was a (grate/great) day! TEC61357
2. I wish we had more (brakes/ breaks) during the day. TEC61357	7. I saw a large ship in the (sea/see). TEC61357
3. The (some/sum) of three plus eight is 11. TEC61357	8. I have a new puppy (to/too)! TEC61357
4. Did you (hear/here) me? TEC61357	9. We (ate/eight) pizza for lunch. TEC61357
5. The wind (blew/blue) very hard during the storm. TEC61357	10. It took me three (hours/ours) to do my homework. TEC61357

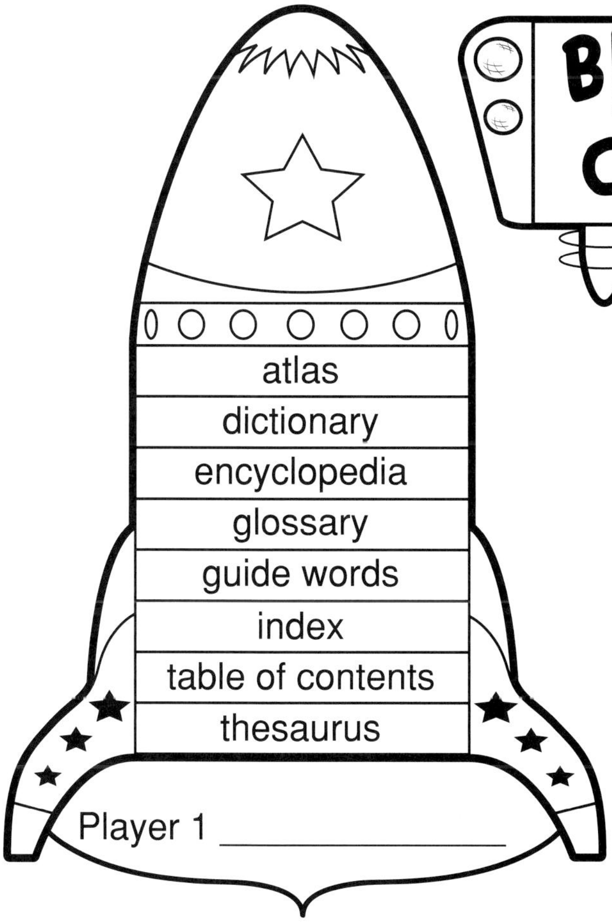

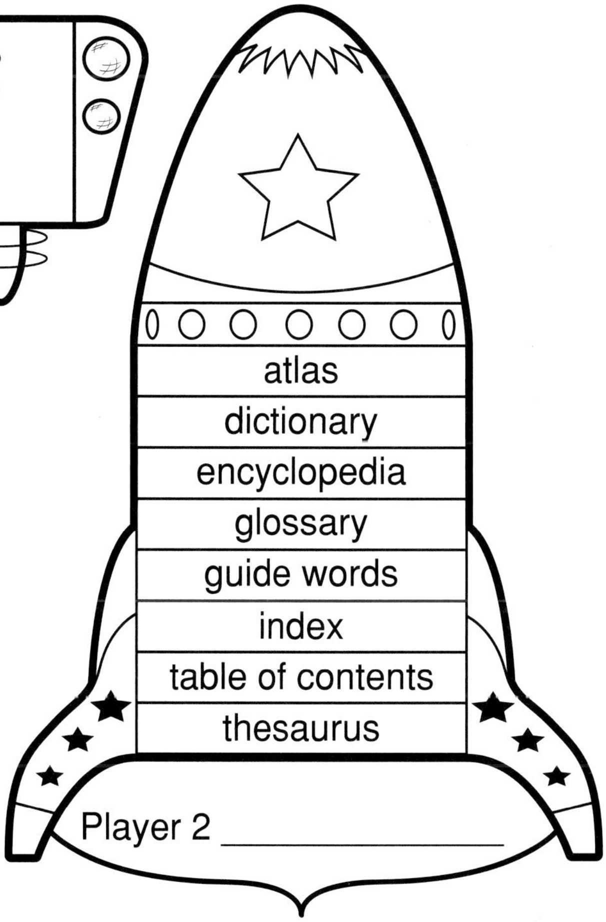

Note to the teacher: Use with "Blast Off" on page 60.

Verb Tense Cards

Use with "Action-Packed Games" on page 59.

Past Tense Yesterday I **cleaned.** TEC61357	Present Tense Today I am **cleaning.** TEC61357	Future Tense Tomorrow I will **clean.** TEC61357
Past Tense Yesterday I **played.** TEC61357	Present Tense Today I am **playing.** TEC61357	Future Tense Tomorrow I will **play.** TEC61357
Past Tense Yesterday I **mailed.** TEC61357	Present Tense Today I am **mailing.** TEC61357	Future Tense Tomorrow I will **mail.** TEC61357
Past Tense Yesterday I **dashed.** TEC61357	Present Tense Today I am **dashing.** TEC61357	Future Tense Tomorrow I will **dash.** TEC61357
Past Tense Yesterday I **watched.** TEC61357	Present Tense Today I am **watching.** TEC61357	Future Tense Tomorrow I will **watch.** TEC61357
Past Tense Yesterday I **collected.** TEC61357	Present Tense Today I am **collecting.** TEC61357	Future Tense Tomorrow I will **collect.** TEC61357
Kaboom! TEC61357	**Kaboom!** TEC61357	**Kaboom!** TEC61357

1 magical fairy TEC61357	2 by the ocean TEC61357	3 A bird lost its way. TEC61357
4 Willy TEC61357	5 last summer TEC61357	6 A spell was cast on a prince. TEC61357
7 Principal Jones TEC61357	8 in a far-off land TEC61357	9 A cat was stuck in a tree. TEC61357
10 Officer Neal TEC61357	11 on the playground TEC61357	12 They were out of money. TEC61357
13 Mrs. Frog TEC61357	14 in a dark forest TEC61357	15 Her house was a mess! TEC61357

Game Cards

Use with "Blast Off" on page 60.

- It is a book.
- It has maps.
- It tells about places on Earth.

TEC61357

- It is a book.
- It has maps.
- It tells about places on Earth.

TEC61357

- It is a book.
- It is arranged in ABC order.
- It tells the meaning of many different words.

TEC61357

- It is a book.
- It is arranged in ABC order.
- It tells the meaning of many different words.

TEC61357

- It is a book.
- It is arranged in ABC order.
- It tells about each subject listed.

TEC61357

- It is a book.
- It is arranged in ABC order.
- It tells about each subject listed.

TEC61357

- It is a book.
- It is arranged in ABC order.
- It names synonyms for each listed word.
- It may also list antonyms for each word.

TEC61357

- It is a book.
- It is arranged in ABC order.
- It names synonyms for each listed word.
- It may also list antonyms for each word.

TEC61357

- It is part of a book.
- It lists key words found in the book.
- It also tells each word's meaning.
- It is often in the back of the book.

TEC61357

- It is part of a book.
- It lists key words found in the book.
- It also tells each word's meaning.
- It is often in the back of the book.

TEC61357

- These are part of a book page.
- There are two words.
- The first word tells the first entry word on the page.
- The second word tells the last entry word on the page.

TEC61357

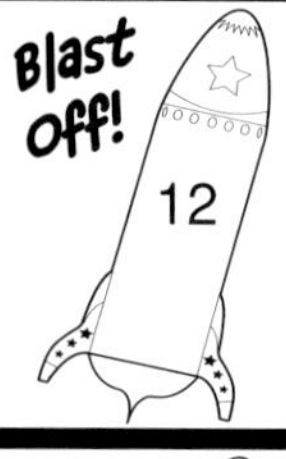

- These are part of a book page.
- There are two words.
- The first word tells the first entry word on the page.
- The second word tells the last entry word on the page.

TEC61357

- It is part of a book.
- It is a list of key words in the book.
- It also tells the page number each word is on.

TEC61357

- It is part of a book.
- It is a list of key words in the book.
- It also tells the page number each word is on.

TEC61357

- It is part of a book.
- It is found at the beginning of the book.
- It shows the chapters or sections of the book.
- It is ordered from the beginning of the book to the end.

TEC61357

- It is part of a book.
- It is found at the beginning of the book.
- It shows the chapters or sections of the book.
- It is ordered from the beginning of the book to the end.

TEC61357

Math GAMES

Math GAMES

Hands-Down Fun

Commutative property

To prepare this partner game, cut out the cards on page 83. Sort the cards by operation; then place each set along with a copy of the answer key on page 95 in a resealable plastic bag. To play, a pair selects a bag, removes the cards, and places them facedown on the playing surface. Player 1 turns over three cards. If all three cards correspond, as shown, then a match has been made, and he keeps the cards. If the cards are not a match, he turns them facedown, and Player 2 takes a turn. Play continues in this manner until all the cards have been matched. The student with more cards wins.

Jean Erickson
Grace Christian School
West Allis, WI

Laura Wagner, Raleigh, NC

Speed Zone

Addition of two- and three-digit numbers

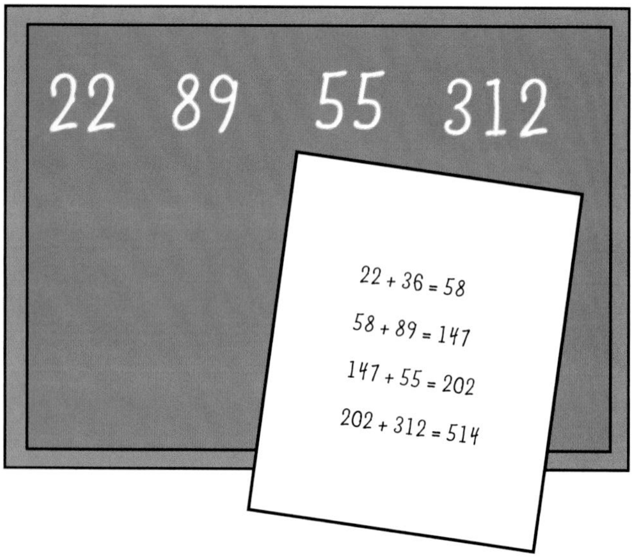

In this fast-paced game, students work in teams to hone their addition skills! Give each group of four a sheet of paper and a pencil. Also, write on the board four different numbers. Begin the game by having each group's Student 1 write the first number on her paper. Then announce a number for her to add to it. She solves the problem and then passes the paper to Student 2. This child checks Student 1's work and then adds the second number on the board to the solution. Students 3 and 4 repeat the process, using different numbers from the board. After all teams finish, check the problems as a class. Award a point to each team that correctly solved all four problems. Then post four new numbers on the board and begin another round.

Laura Wagner

Math GAMES

Mystery Number

Two-digit addition and subtraction

The only materials needed for this partner game are a deck of cards (face cards removed), paper, and a pencil! Before play begins, explain to students that each ace equals one. To play:

1. Player 1 writes a two-digit number other than 50 on a piece of paper and then turns the paper facedown.
2. Player 2 asks, “Is the mystery number greater than or less than 50?” and Player 1 responds.
3. Player 2 takes a card from the deck and, based on Player 1’s response, either adds the card’s value to or subtracts it from 50.
4. Player 2 asks Player 1 if the resulting answer is the mystery number. If it is, the round ends and the students switch roles. If it is not, Player 2 continues taking cards from the deck and adding or subtracting the face values to each new sum or difference until she determines the mystery number.

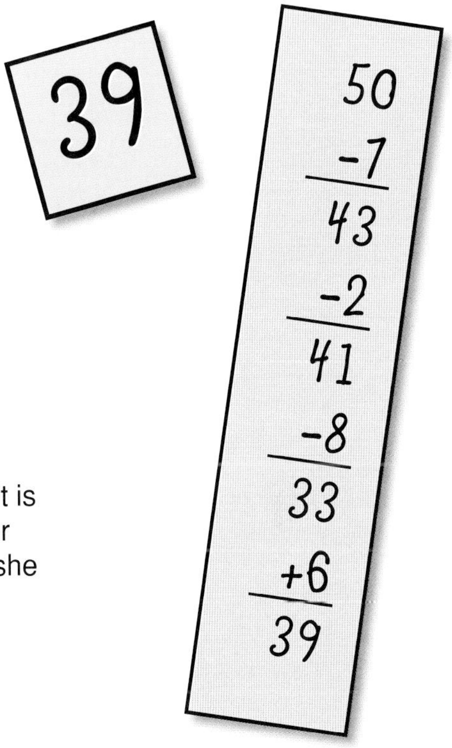

Stacie Wright
Millington School
Millington, NJ

Spin and Solve

Skill review

Looking for a partner game that reinforces any math skill? Try this. Make an answer key by programming a copy of a math reproducible with the answers. Place at a center the key, a copy of the spinner on page 87, blank copies of the reproducible, a pencil, and a paper clip. Player 1 spins the spinner and reads the direction aloud. For each problem solved, his partner checks the key. For each correct answer, the player writes his initials next to the problem. He erases any incorrect answers. Students take turns as time allows. The player with more initialed answers wins.

Mary Burgess
Howell Valley Elementary
West Plains, MO

Take a Swat

Skill review

Follow up an independent practice sheet with this fun game! Write the answers to the skill sheet's problems on the board and then divide the class into two teams. Give one member of each team a clean flyswatter and invite the two students to stand with their backs to the board, each holding her flyswatter and her paper. After you read a problem aloud, the students turn and swat the correct answer. The first child to do so earns a point for her team; then both students return to their teams. Repeat with two new players. The team with more points at the end of play wins.

Brandon Beard
Queen's Creek Elementary
Swansboro, NC

Valuable Practice

Basic facts

To prepare this partner game, give each twosome ten yellow circles (coins) and flash cards. Player 1 reads a problem from a flash card to Player 2. If Player 2 gives the correct answer, he takes a coin. Players take turns reading and responding until all ten coins are distributed. The player with more coins wins. **To make this an independent game,** prepare a class supply of large coins. The student takes ten flash cards, challenges himself to correctly solve each problem, and then checks the answer. He writes any missed problems on a coin for practice at home or during class free time.

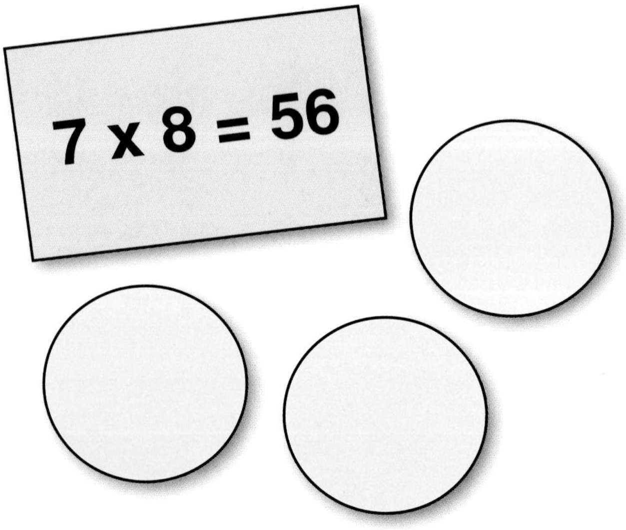

Laura Wagner
Bais Menachem Hebrew Academy
Austin, TX

High Roller

Multiplying, adding

To get this partner game rolling, give each student pair two dice and a copy of the recording sheet on page 88. Player 1 rolls the dice and multiplies the values together. She records her product on the sheet, then rolls again. After recording the second product, she adds the products together. Then Player 2 rolls the dice and records his totals. The player with the higher sum circles the number and wins the round. The duo continues in this manner until all rounds have been played or time is called. The player who wins more rounds wins the game.

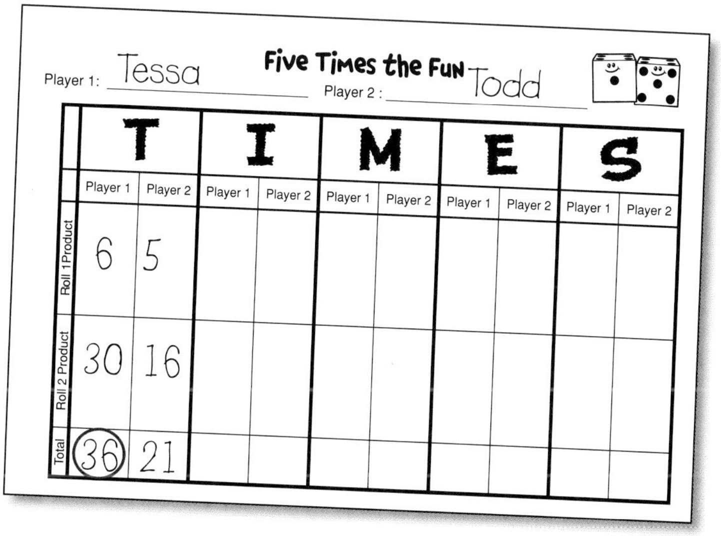

Five Times the Fun

Player 1: Tessa Player 2: Todd

	T		I		M		E		S	
	Player 1	Player 2	Player 1	Player 2	Player 1	Player 2	Player 1	Player 2	Player 1	Player 2
Roll 1 Product	6	5								
Roll 2 Product	30	16								
Total	36	21								

Stacie Wright
Millington School
Millington, NJ

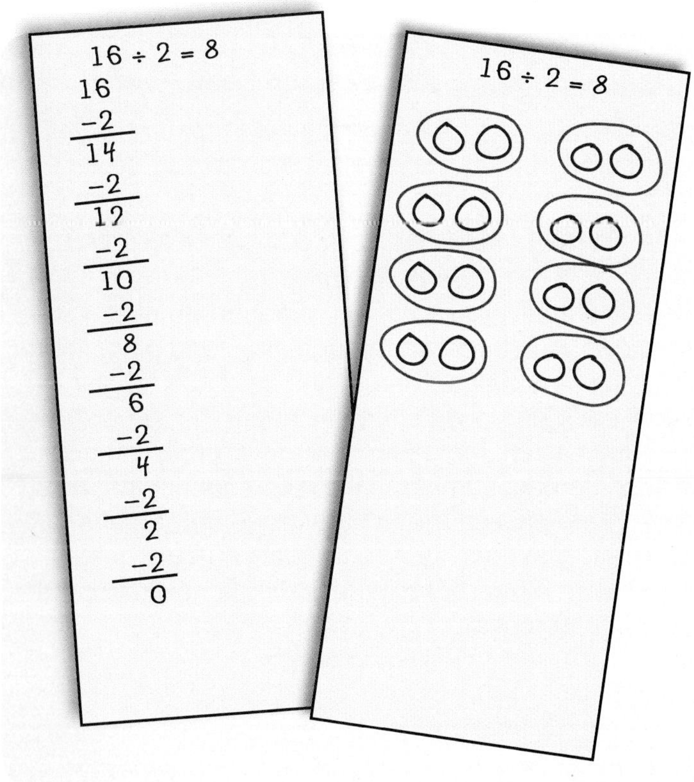

Duplicate Answers

Division concepts

To prepare this class game, write a division problem on the board; then assign each student one of two strategies to solve it, such as repeated subtraction or drawing a picture. On your signal, direct students to use their assigned strategies to solve the problem and then turn their papers over. When all students appear to be done, call on one student from each strategy group to reveal her results to the class. If both students reveal the same correct quotient, award the class a point. Write a new problem on the board and continue in this manner until a predetermined number of points has been awarded.

Got Your Number

Reading numbers and number words

To begin this partner game, have students cut apart a copy of the cards and gameboards from page 89 and then stack the cards facedown. Also give the players a copy of the answer key on page 95. To begin, Player 1 turns a card over, looks at the number, and checks his gameboard for the matching number word. If he finds a match, the student places the card on the matching square and his partner checks his answer. If he does not find a match, the student returns the card to the bottom of the stack and his turn ends. Play continues until one player's gameboard is filled. If time allows, students switch gameboards and play again.

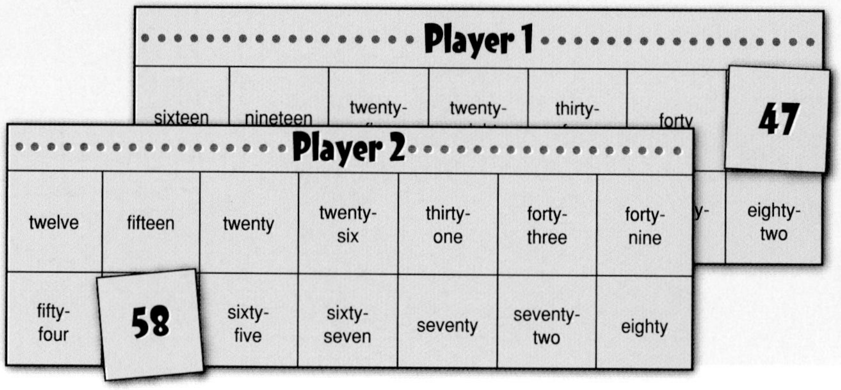

adapted from an idea by Anna Hicks
W. R. Odell Elementary
Concord, NC

Quick and Easy Game! See pages 90 and 91 for a reproducible partner game on ROUNDING to the nearest ten!

Moving Toward Multiplication

Skip-counting

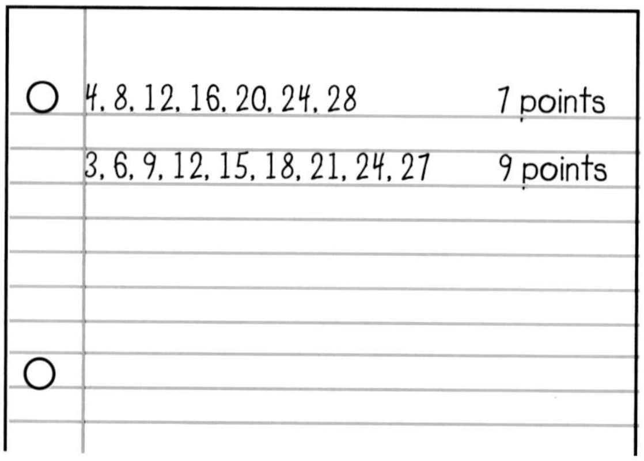

Give each small group a sheet of paper. Shuffle eight playing cards, numbers two through nine, and place them facedown along a ledge. Reveal one card and have a student in each group write the card's number on a sheet of paper. He passes the paper to another group member, who writes the next number in the skip-counting pattern. The paper gets passed around the group until time is called. Award one point for each correct number in the pattern. Play another round by revealing a new card and repeating the process.

Laura Wagner
Bais Menachem Hebrew Academy
Austin, TX

Rolling Along

Understanding place value, writing numbers

Before the game, create a set of index cards labeled as shown for each group of four students. Start by giving each group a die, a set of cards, and a sheet of paper. Have each child draw a card. The student who has the recorder card draws a three-column place-value chart like the one shown. Each student with a place-value card rolls the die, in turn, and holds it up for the recorder to list on his paper in the corresponding column. After each number is recorded, the recorder reads the three-digit number aloud. Then the students switch cards and repeat the process. Groups continue working in this manner until time is called. If desired, challenge students to make the largest and smallest numbers possible for each roll.

Jean Erickson
Grace Christian School
West Allis, WI

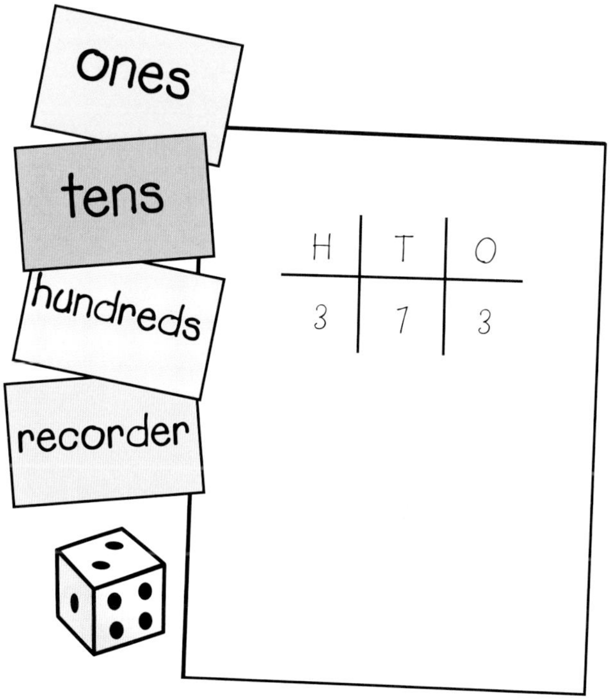

Got It Covered!

Reading numbers, identifying the value of digits

This versatile partner game helps students work with numbers to 999 or 9,999. In advance, give each student pair two paper clips, a supply of game markers, and a copy of the spinner card on page 92 that best suits your reinforcement needs. Also guide each child to fold a sheet of paper to make 16 sections and then unfold it. Have him program each section with a different number that is less than the number on the spinner card.

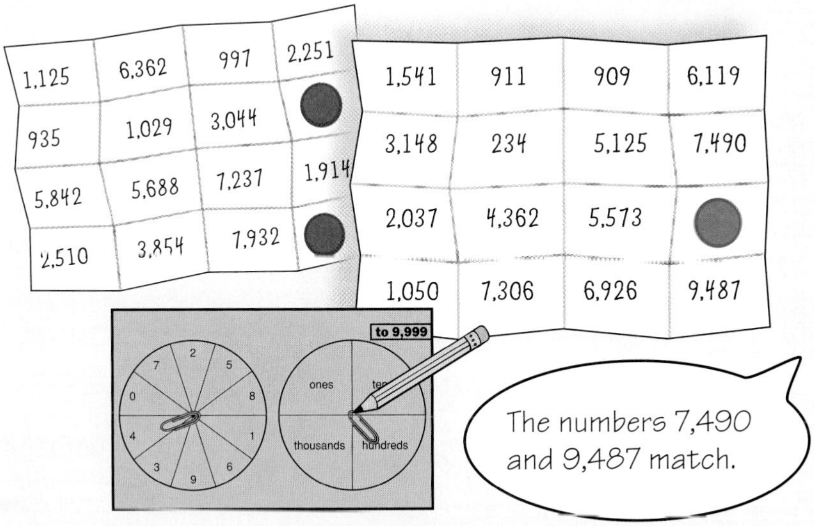

To play, Player 1 uses a paper clip and pencil to spin each spinner. He looks for numbers on his gameboard that match the two clues; for example, if he spins "3" and "hundreds," he looks for numbers that have a three in the hundreds place. Player 1 reads aloud any numbers that match, then covers each one with a game marker. If no numbers match, Player 1's turn is over. Then Player 2 takes a turn in a similar manner. Students alternate play until one student has covered all of his sections.

Time Flies

Finding elapsed time

To prepare this partner game, cut out the game cards from page 93 and place them in a resealable plastic bag. Place the gameboard from page 85 and the bag at a center, along with a pencil, a paper clip, a manipulative clock (pattern on page 93), and two game markers.

To play, Player 1 removes the cards from the bag and places them facedown in a stack. Then he takes the top card and reads aloud the times on the card. Player 2 uses the manipulative clock to determine the trip time and then announces her answer. Player 1 checks the answer. If Player 2 is correct, she uses the pencil and paper clip to spin and then moves her game marker accordingly. If her answer is incorrect, Player 1 returns the card to the bottom of the stack. Players alternate turns, and the first player to reach Finish is the winner.

Jean Erickson
Grace Christian School
West Allis, WI,

Making a Bundle

Counting coins with mixed values

This fun variation of War challenges student pairs to look out for big money! Use coin stamps or coin clip art to program an even number of index cards with different money amounts. To begin, each player receives half of the deck with the cards facedown in a stack. At a predetermined signal, both players turn over their top cards. The player with the greater coin value takes both cards. If both cards show equal values, each player takes the top card off his pile and places it faceup on the card at play. The player with the greater value takes all four cards. Play continues in this manner until one player has all the cards or until time is called and the player with more cards wins.

Stacie Wright
Millington School
Millington, NJ

Screened-in Shapes

Identifying patterns using concrete objects

This partner game adds a mathematical slant to 20 Questions. First, give each student a matching supply of pattern blocks. Pair students and have Player 1 fold a piece of card stock in half as shown. Next, have Player 1 create a pattern with her blocks, using the folded paper as a workmat and a screen. Then challenge Player 2 to determine the hidden pattern by asking a yes-or-no question, such as "Is the first shape in the pattern a triangle? " or "Is it an ABC pattern?" After hearing Player 1's response, Player 2 uses his pattern blocks to replicate the hidden pattern. He shows his work to Player 1, who identifies which blocks are placed correctly. Player 2 continues in this manner until he determines the pattern or until he has asked 20 questions. Then players switch roles.

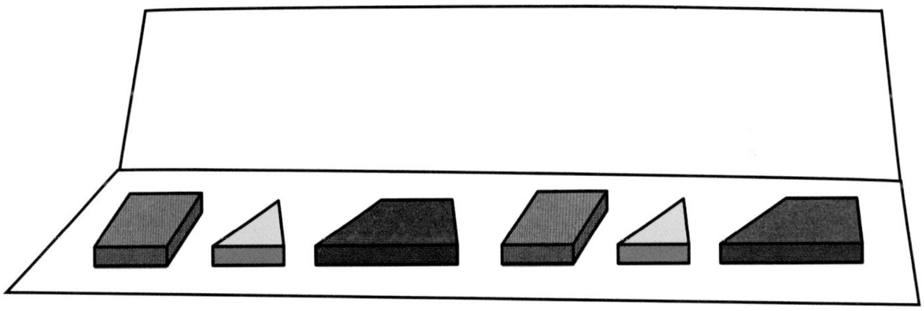

Stacie Stone Davis
Lima, NY

Spy Eyes

Identifying fractions

Looking for a quick, fun, and engaging fraction game? Then this is the one for you! To begin, secretly identify a fraction occurring in your room. For example, you might see that three of your four computers are on. Then announce to students, "I spy with my fraction eye, the fraction three-fourths." Students ask yes-or-no questions to figure out what you are referring to. If a child asks a question that equals the fraction you named but does not represent the objects you are looking for, accept the answer and start a new round. However, if a child correctly identifies the objects you are thinking of, that child takes over the role as spy and starts a new round.

David Green
North Shore Country Day School
Winnetka, IL

Math GAMES

Leapin' Lions

Measurement

To introduce this small-group activity, tell students that an African lion can leap a distance of up to 36 feet, or about the length of two minivans. Next, have one group member draw a table like the one shown. The group members designate a starting line; then each child, in turn, leaps forward from the line. The other group members use rulers or yardsticks to measure and record the distance leapt. Then the child determines the difference between the distance of his leap and the lion's. After each group member has had a turn, have students share their results with the rest of the class.

Stacie Wright
Millington School
Millington, NJ

Lion's Leap	Leaper	Distance	Difference
36 feet	Landon	3 feet	36 – 3 = 33 feet
36 feet	Lisel	4 feet	36 – 4 = 32 feet
36 feet	Leander		

Walk the Line

Area and perimeter

Use the classic game of musical chairs to introduce the concept of perimeter and area. Place two rows of three chairs back-to-back and put a rectangular border of tape around the group of chairs. Have six students stand on the border and face the same direction; then start the music. Guide students to walk on the tape and softly repeat the word *perimeter* until the music stops. Then direct each student to sit on a chair and say, "Area." Provide time for each student to have a turn.

Karen Slattery
Marie of the Incarnation School
Bradford, Ontario, Canada

Game Cards

Use with "Hands-Down Fun" on page 74.

7 + 9 =	3 + 7 =	2 + 4 =	8 + 5 =
9 + 7 =	7 + 3 =	4 + 2 =	5 + 8 =
16	10	6	13
6 + 1 =	3 + 8 =	4 + 5 =	8 + 7 =
1 + 6 =	8 + 3 =	5 + 4 =	7 + 8 =
7	11	9	15
2 x 9 =	3 x 4 =	6 x 5 =	4 x 7 =
9 x 2 =	4 x 3 =	5 x 6 =	7 x 4 =
18	12	30	28
3 x 6 =	5 x 8 =	2 x 6 =	4 x 5 =
6 x 3 =	8 x 5 =	6 x 2 =	5 x 4 =
18	40	12	20

TEC61357	TEC61357	TEC61357	TEC61357
TEC61357	TEC61357	TEC61357	TEC61357
TEC61357	TEC61357	TEC61357	TEC61357
TEC61357	TEC61357	TEC61357	TEC61357
TEC61357	TEC61357	TEC61357	TEC61357
TEC61357	TEC61357	TEC61357	TEC61357
TEC61357	TEC61357	TEC61357	TEC61357
TEC61357	TEC61357	TEC61357	TEC61357
TEC61357	TEC61357	TEC61357	TEC61357
TEC61357	TEC61357	TEC61357	TEC61357
TEC61357	TEC61357	TEC61357	TEC61357
TEC61357	TEC61357	TEC61357	TEC61357

 Partner Game: Use with "Time Flies" on page 80.

Spinner Pattern

Use with "Spin and Solve" on page 75.

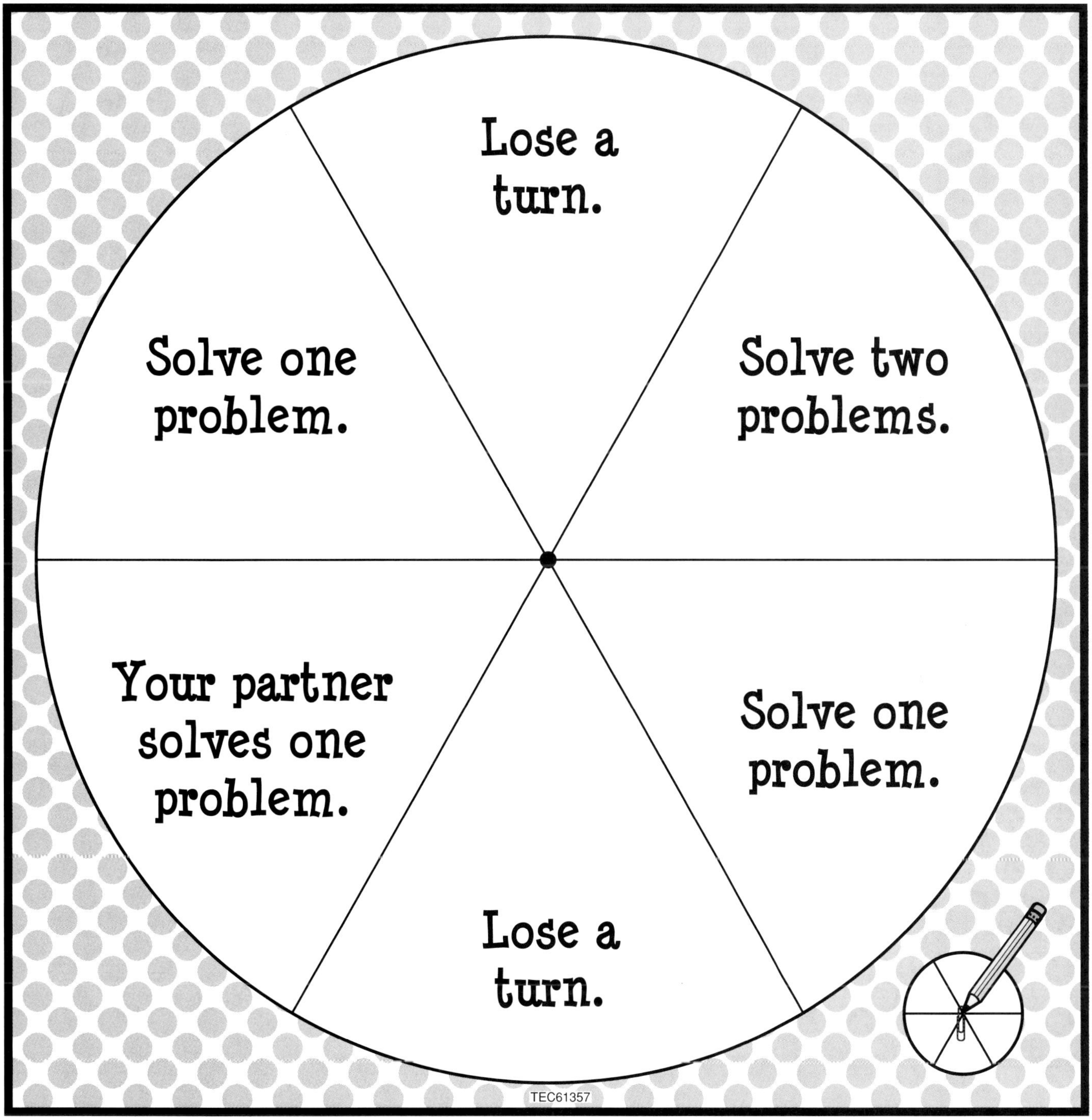

Five Times the Fun

Player 1: ______________________ Player 2 : ______________________

	T		I		M		E		S	
	Player 1	Player 2	Player 1	Player 2	Player 1	Player 2	Player 1	Player 2	Player 1	Player 2
Roll 1 Product										
Roll 2 Product										
Total										

Note to the teacher: Use with "High Roller" on page 77.

Player 1

sixteen	nineteen	twenty-five	twenty-eight	thirty-four	forty	forty-seven
fifty-	fifty-	sixty-	sixty-	seventy-	seventy-	eighty-two

Player 2

twelve	fifteen	twenty	twenty-six	thirty-one	forty-three	forty-nine
fifty-four	fifty-eight	sixty-five	sixty-seven	seventy	seventy-two	eighty

12 TEC61357	15 TEC61357	16 TEC61357	19 TEC61357	20 TEC61357	25 TEC61357	26 TEC61357
28 TEC61357	31 TEC61357	34 TEC61357	40 TEC61357	43 TEC61357	47 TEC61357	49 TEC61357
52 TEC61357	54 TEC61357	56 TEC61357	58 TEC61357	61 TEC61357	65 TEC61357	66 TEC61357
67 TEC61357	70 TEC61357	72 TEC61357	73 TEC61357	79 TEC61357	80 TEC61357	82 TEC61357

Names ______________________________ Date ______________

Rounding to the nearest ten

Web Race!

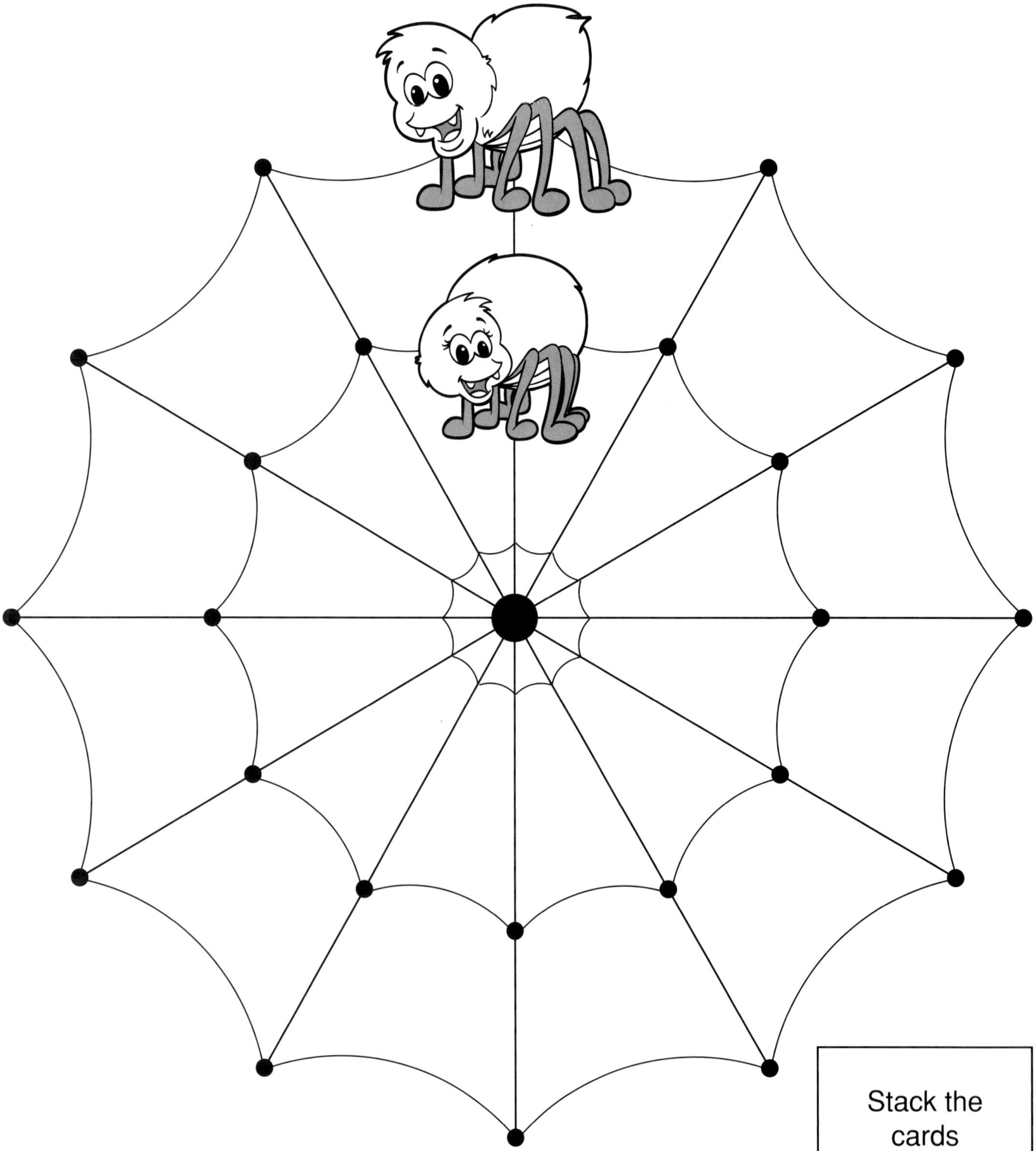

Stack the cards facedown.

Reproducible Math Game: Make a copy of this page and page 91 for each student pair. Also provide each pair with two game markers, such as Unifix cubes, paper clips, or discarded highlighter caps.

Web Race!

Directions for two players:

1. Put your game marker on a spider. Stack the cards facedown on the gameboard.
2. When it's your turn, take the top card. Say the number. Round it to the nearest ten.
3. Have your partner check the key.
   - If you are correct, move one dot to the right. Return the card to the bottom of the stack.
   - If you are incorrect, return the card to the bottom of the stack.
4. The first player to move his or her marker around the web and back to his or her spider wins.

TEC61357

Web Race!
Answer Key

A. 10	B. 20	C. 50
D. 50	E. 80	F. 40
G. 30	H. 80	I. 30
J. 100	K. 20	L. 70
M. 10	N. 10	O. 90
P. 50	Q. 90	R. 80
S. 40	T. 60	U. 20
V. 70	W. 60	X. 30

TEC61357

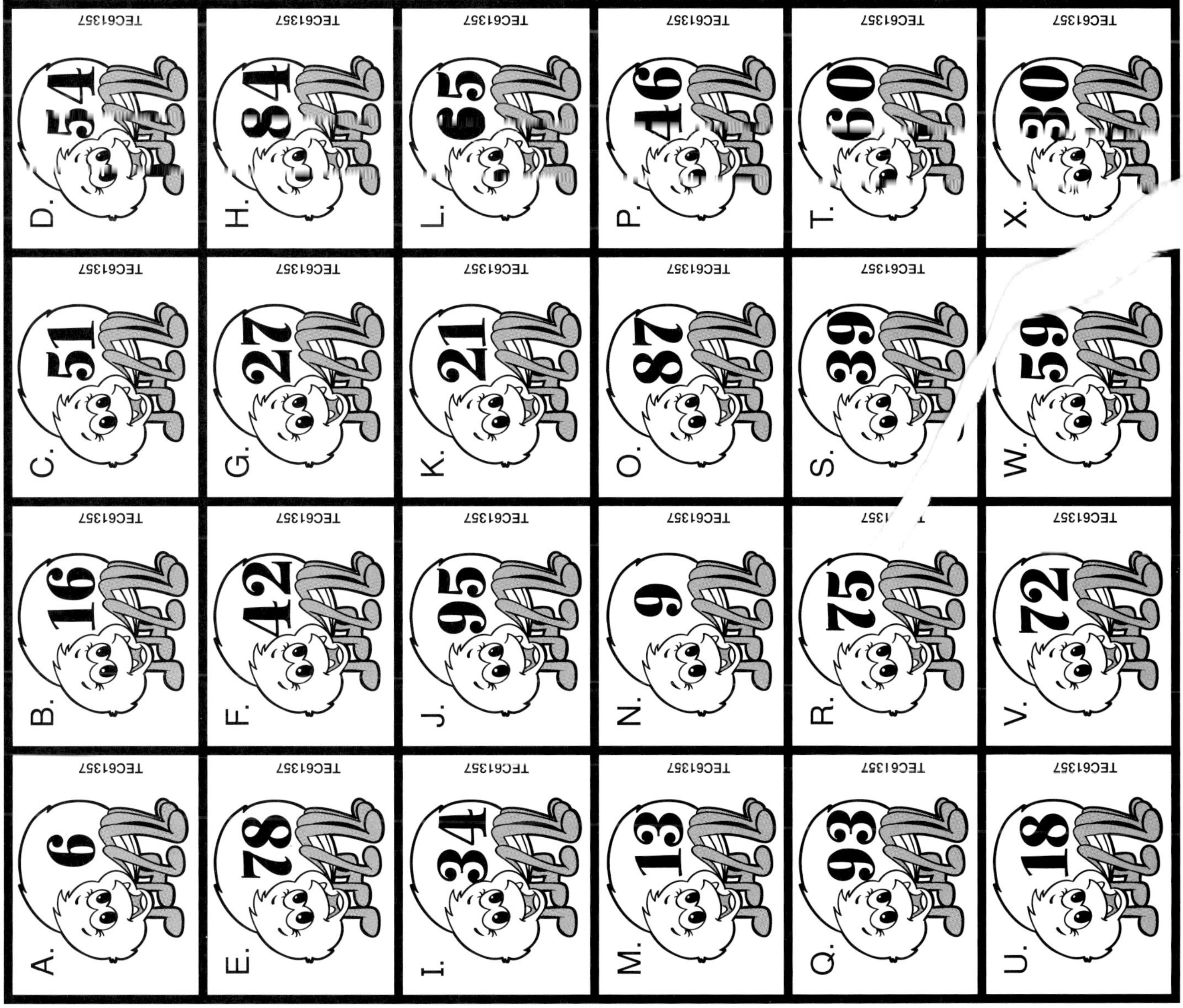

Note to the teacher: Use with the gameboard on page 90.

Spinner Cards

Use with "Got It Covered!" on page 79.

to 999

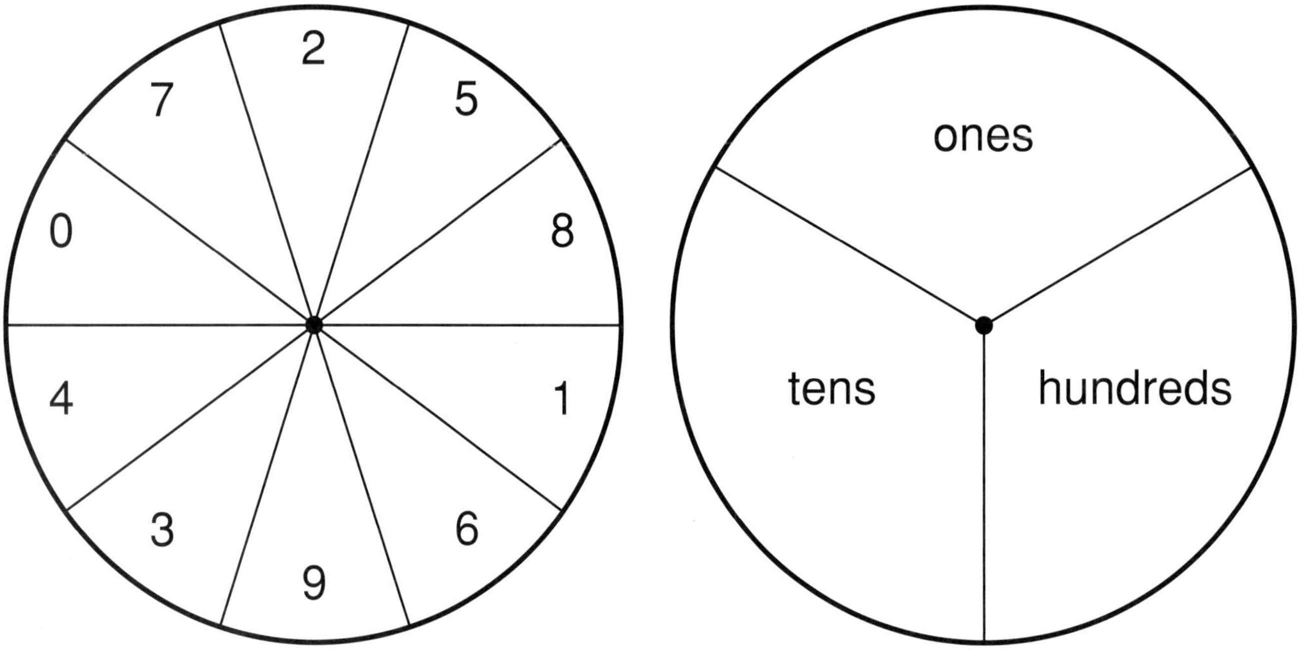

TEC61357

to 9,999

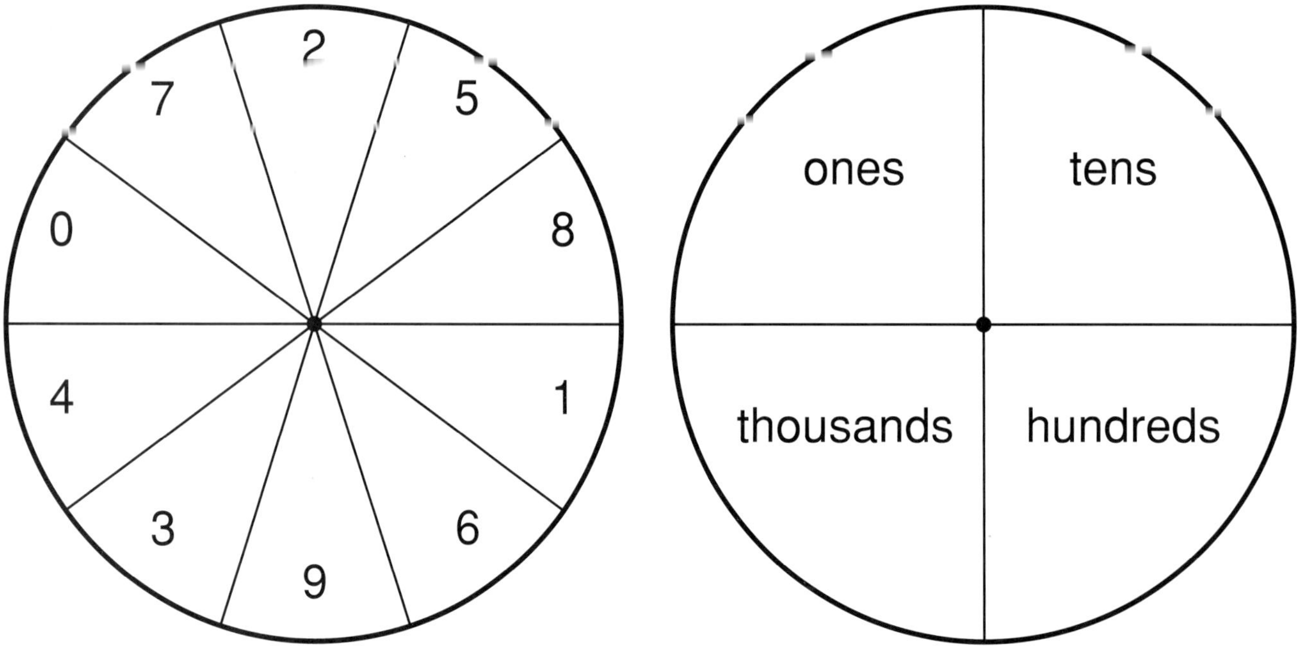

TEC61357

Clock Patterns and Game Cards

Use with “Time Flies” on page 80.

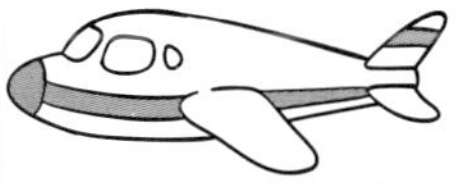 Leave **8:30 AM** Arrive **9:25 AM** Trip time = 55 min. TEC61357	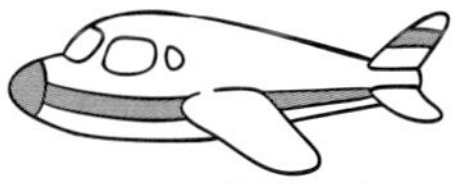 Leave **3:20 PM** Arrive **4:30 PM** Trip time = 1 hr., 10 min. TEC61357	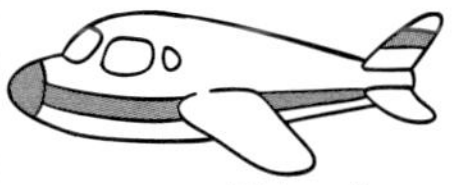 Leave **5:55 PM** Arrive **7:30 PM** Trip time = 1 hr., 35 min. TEC61357
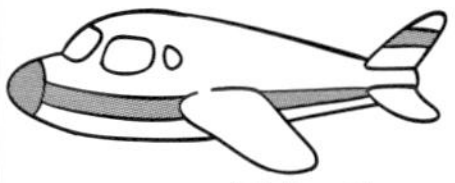 Leave **6:15 PM** Arrive **7:35 PM** Trip time = 1 hr., 20 min. TEC61357	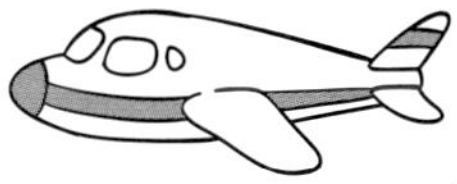 Leave **8:30 AM** Arrive **9:30 AM** Trip time = 1 hr. TEC61357	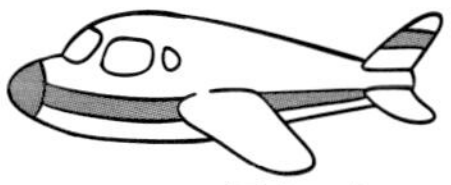 Leave **7:10 PM** Arrive **9:30 PM** Trip time = 2 hr., 20 min. TEC61357
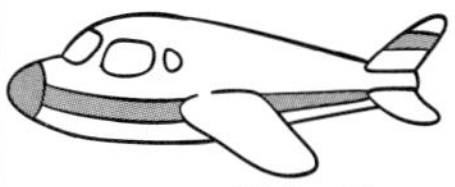 Leave **11:20 AM** Arrive **12:30 AM** Trip time = 1 hr., 10 min. TEC61357	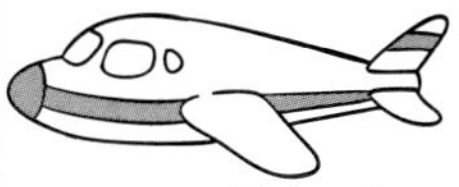 Leave **10:00 AM** Arrive **11:30 AM** Trip time = 1 hr., 30 min. TEC61357	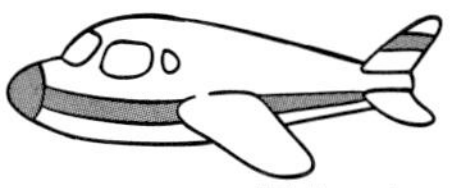 Leave **5:25 PM** Arrive **6:30 PM** Trip time = 1 hr., 5 min. TEC61357
 Leave **3:00 PM** Arrive **4:40 PM** Trip time = 1 hr., 40 min. TEC43034	 Leave **1:05 PM** Arrive **2:20 PM** Trip time = 1 hr., 15 min. TEC43034	 Leave **8:35 AM** Arrive **10:10 AM** Trip time = 1 hr., 35 min. TEC61357
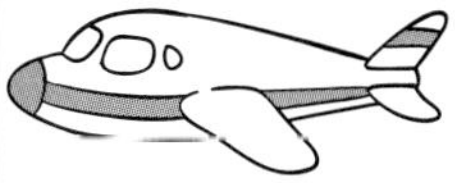 Leave **6:00 PM** Arrive **7:05 PM** Trip time = 1 hr., 5 min. TEC61357	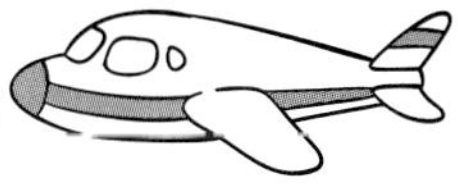 Leave **5:45 PM** Arrive **7:10 PM** Trip time = 1 hr., 25 min. TEC61357	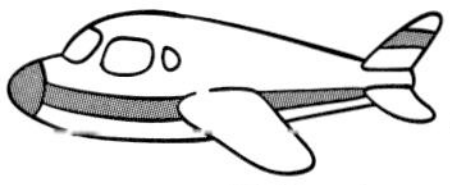 Leave **9:25 AM** Arrive **11:20 AM** Trip time = 1 hr., 55 min. TEC61357
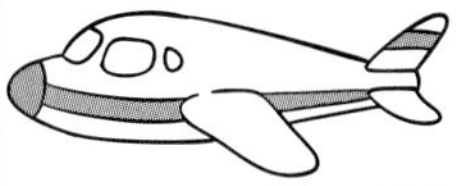 Leave **10:20 AM** Arrive **11:15 AM** Trip time = 55 min. TEC61357	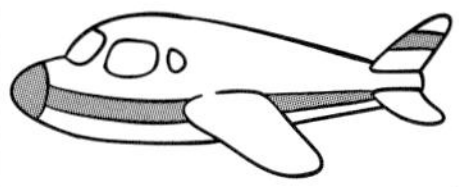 Leave **2:40 PM** Arrive **3:40 PM** Trip time = 1 hr. TEC61357	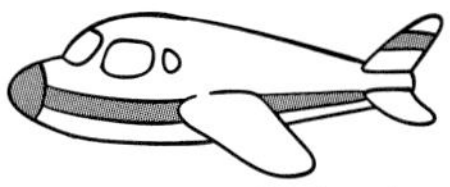 Leave **4:00 PM** Arrive **6:05 PM** Trip time = 2 hr., 5 min. TEC61357

Answer Keys

Page 9
"Words With Prefixes"
Answer Key

pre- preread, premade, prewrite, pregame

re- recall, replay, reread, remade, retell, rewrite

un- unmade, unhealthy, unkind, unlucky, unhappy, unhurt

TEC61357

Page 36
"Larry the Landscaper"
Answer Key

Project A: 28 ft.

Project B: 19 ft.

Project C: 45 sq. ft.

Project D: 36 sq. ft.

Project E: 22 ft.

Project F: 60 sq. ft.

TEC61357

Page 63
"To the Lemonade Stand!"
Answer Key

1. lemons
2. teeth
3. kisses
4. beaches
5. hills
6. mice
7. feet
8. berries
9. men
10. bushes
11. geese
12. ladies
13. children
14. ponies
15. women
16. bunches
17. parties
18. boxes
19. boys
20. mixes

TEC61357

Page 61
"A Place to Call Home"
Player 2
Answer Key

(Player 1 checks.)

1. brave, fearless
2. catch, trap
3. late, overdue
4. real, true
5. cottage, house
6. shout, yell
7. fast, quick
8. tired, worn-out
9. snout, nose

TEC61357

Page 61
"A Place to Call Home"
Player 1
Answer Key

(Player 2 checks.)

1. woman, lady
2. slow, poky
3. run, jog
4. little, small
5. sly, sneaky
6. old, aged
7. chase, follow
8. wet, soaked
9. toss, throw

TEC61357

Page 60
"Important Ingredients"
Answer Key

Character: 1, 4, 7, 10, 13
Setting: 2, 5, 8, 11, 14
Problem: 3, 6, 9, 12, 15

TEC61357

Page 65
"Flipping for Stories"
Answer Key

Mystery: 1 or 2, 4, 7, 10
Fantasy: 1 or 2, 5, 8, 11
Biography: 3, 6, 9, 12

TEC61357

Page 60
"Blast Off"
Answer Key

atlas: 1, 2

dictionary: 3, 4

encyclopedia: 5, 6

thesaurus: 7, 8

glossary: 9, 10

guide words: 11, 12

index: 13, 14

table of contents: 15, 16

TEC61357

Page 74
"Hands-Down Fun"
Answer Key
Blue Cards

7 + 9 =	6 + 1 =
9 + 7 =	1 + 6 =
16	7
3 + 7 =	3 + 8 =
7 + 3 =	8 + 3 =
10	11
2 + 4 =	4 + 5 =
4 + 2 =	5 + 4 =
6	9
8 + 5 =	8 + 7 =
5 + 8 =	7 + 8 =
13	15

TEC61357

Page 74
"Hands-Down Fun"
Answer Key
Yellow Cards

2 x 9 =	3 x 6 =
9 x 2 =	6 x 3 =
18	18
3 x 4 =	5 x 8 =
4 x 3 =	8 x 5 =
12	40
6 x 5 =	2 x 6 =
5 x 6 =	6 x 2 =
30	12
4 x 7 =	4 x 5 =
7 x 4 =	5 x 4 =
28	20

TEC61357

Page 78
"Got Your Number"
Answer Key
for Player 1 Board
(Player 2 checks.)

sixteen = 16
nineteen = 19
twenty-five = 25
twenty-eight = 28
thirty-four = 34
forty = 40
forty-seven = 47
fifty-two = 52
fifty-six = 56
sixty-one = 61
sixty-six = 66
seventy-three = 73
seventy-nine = 79
eighty-two = 82

TEC61357

Page 78
"Got Your Number"
Answer Key
for Player 2 Board
(Player 1 checks.)

twelve = 12
fifteen = 15
twenty = 20
twenty-six = 26
thirty-one = 31
forty-three = 43
forty-nine = 49
fifty-four = 54
fifty-eight = 58
sixty-five = 65
sixty-seven = 67
seventy = 70
seventy-two = 72
eighty = 80

TEC61357

Skills Index

A

addition
- doubles and near doubles, 28
- products, 77, 88
- two- and three-digit numbers, 74
- two-digit numbers, 75

alphabetical order, 9

C

capitalization
- places, holidays, special events, times in history, 6, 13
- rules, 56

compound words, 56, 68

D

division,
- concepts, 77
- step-by-step center, 37

F

fractions
- and decimals, 35, 41
- comparing, 35
- identifying, 81

G

geometry
- perimeter and area, 36, 49, 82
- polygons, 36, 50
- symmetry, 35, 48

H

homophones, 8, 22, 57, 69

I

inflectional endings, 8, 54

M

math
- basic facts, 76
- commutative property, 74, 83, 95
- computation skills, 29
- elapsed time, 80, 85, 93
- estimation, 33, 47
- expanded form, 31
- identifying the value of digits, 79, 92
- place value, 31, 39, 79
- probability, 32, 46
- problem solving, 32, 45
- rounding to the nearest ten, 90–91
- skill review, 75, 76, 87
- skip-counting, 78
- using < and >, 28, 43

measurement
- length, 82
- weight with nonstandard units, 33, 47

money
- adding, 34, 48
- coin values, 34
- counting coins with mixed values, 80

multiplication, 29, 30, 44, 77, 88

N

nouns
- common and proper, 58
- plural, 4, 63

P

patterning, identifying using concrete objects, 81

patterns
- compound word game and answer key cards, 68
- detail cards, 25
- elapsed time clock and game cards, 93
- greater- and less-than cards, 43
- homophone cards, 22
- homophone sentence cards, 69
- jewels, 43
- knight, 20
- math spinner, 87
- notepad pages, 49
- number and number word game cards and gameboards, 89
- order pad, 48
- place value spinner cards, 92
- polygon riddles and answer key, 50
- prefix cube, 23
- probability booklet pages, 46
- punctuation cards, 21
- reference material game cards, 72
- rounding to the nearest ten direction, game, and answer key cards, 91
- story elements gameboard and game cards, 71
- story problem cards, 45
- sun cards, 44
- verb tense cards, 70
- word cards, 24
- word strip, 20
- writing labels, 24

phonics
- blends, digraphs, and vowel pairs, 52
- onsets and rimes, 4
- using blends and word families, 52, 67

prefixes, 9, 23

prefixes and suffixes, 57

punctuation
- adding missing commas, 7
- identifying correct, 55
- using correct end marks, 7, 21

R

reading
- comprehension, 12, 17
- details from text, 11, 25
- forms of literature, 65
- numbers, 79
- numbers and number words, 78, 89, 95
- recognizing appropriate inflection, 55
- recognizing reference materials and their parts, 60, 69, 72
- story elements, 60, 71
- text-to-text connections, 12, 26

ready-to-use
- box and crayon cards, 39
- capitalization sorting mat and cards, 13
- commutative property cards, 83
- comprehension dice, 17
- division, 37
- elapsed time gameboard, 85
- forms of literature, 65
- fraction bar and decimal cards, 41
- plural nouns, 63
- suffixes center cards and mat, 15
- synonyms, 61

reproducibles
- blends and word families grid, 67
- estimation recording sheet, 47
- measuring weight with nonstandard units recording sheet, 47
- multiplying, adding recording sheet, 88
- prefix recording sheet, 23
- reference material recording sheet, 69
- rounding to the nearest ten, 90
- spelling, 19
- symmetry recording sheet, 48
- text-to-text connections, 26

S

sentences, creating with meaning, 58

sight words, 6, 20

spelling, 5, 19, 53

subtraction, two-digit numbers, 75

synonyms, 61

V

verbs
- adding *-s* and *-es*, 59
- tenses, 59, 70

W

word skills
- order, 11
- recognition, 54
- review, 53

writing
- descriptive, 10, 24
- numbers, 79
- questions, 10